A Palestinian author and columnist, Marwan Bishara is also an Israeli citizen from Nazareth. He is a lecturer at the American University of Paris and a research fellow at the Ecole des Hautes Etudes en Sciences Sociales. Besides having a number of publications to his name, he writes for a variety of newspapers, including the *International Herald Tribune* (Paris), *Le Figaro* (Paris), *Le Monde Diplomatique* (Paris), *La Vanguardia* (Barcelona) *Al Hayat* (London), and *WOZ* (Zurich).

To Assil Hassan Asleh 18 years, Ala'a Khaled Nassar 18, Rami Hatem Ghara 21, Ramez Abbas Bushnaq 24, Eyad Sobhi Lawabny 26, Omar Muhammed Akkawi 42, Wissam Yazbak 25, Walid Abu Saleh 21, Muhammad Ghaleb Khamayseh 19, Ahmed Siyyam Jabareen 18, Muhammed Ibrahim Jabareen 24, Emad Ghanaym 25, Misleh Abu Jared 14 — all young Palestinian citizens of the state of Israel assassinated by Israeli snipers and security forces at the beginning of October 2000.

PALESTINE/ISRAEL: PEACE OR APARTHEID

Occupation, Terrorism and the Future

Marwan Bishara

Foreword by Richard Falk

ZED BOOKS
London & New York

SPEARHEAD
South Africa

FERNWOOD PUBLISHING
Halifax, Nova Scotia

Palestine/Israel: Peace or Apartheid: Occupation, Terrorism and the Future
was first published in 2001 by Zed Books Ltd, 7, Cynthia Street, London N1
9JF, UK and Room 400, 175 Fifth Avenue, New York, NY 10010, USA under
the title *Palestine/Israel: Peace or Apartheid: Prospects for Resolving the Conflict*

www.zedbooks.demon.co.uk

Second Updated Edition 2002

Distributed in the United States exclusively by Palgrave, a division of St
Martin's Press, LLC, 175 Fifth Avenue, New York, 10010

Published in Canada by Fernwood Publishing Ltd, PO Box 9409, Station A,
Halifax, Nova Scotia, B3K 5S3

Published in South Africa by Spearhead, a division of New Africa Books,
PO Box 23408, Claremont 7735

Published in Jerusalem by The Bookshop, P.O. Box 1603, Jerusalem

Copyright © Marwan Bishara, 2001
French copyright © Editions la Decouverte & Syros, Paris, France 2001

Typeset by Kathryn Perry, Brighton
Cover design by Andrew Corbett

Printed and bound in the United Kingdom by Cox & Wyman, Reading

A catalogue record for this book is available from the British Library
US CIP is available from the Library of Congress

National Library of Canada Cataloguing in Publication Data

Bishara, Marwan
*Palestine/Israel: peace or apartheid: occupation, terrorism and the future / Marwan
Bishara. -- 2nd ed.*

Includes bibliographical references and index. ISBN 1-55266-097-4

1. Arab-Israeli conflict--1993- --Peace. 2. Al-Aqsa Intifada, 2000-. 3.Israel--Politics
and government-. I. Title.

DS119.76.B58 2002   956.05'3   C2002-903554-6

ISBNs
South Africa 0-86486-597-X
Canada 1-55266-097-4 pb
Rest of the world 1 84277 272 4 hb   1 84277 273 2 pb

CONTENTS

v

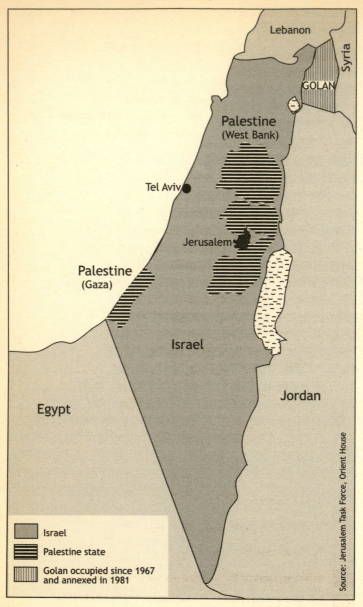

Source: Jerusalem Task Force, Orient House

Israel's Camp David II Proposals for a Palestinian State

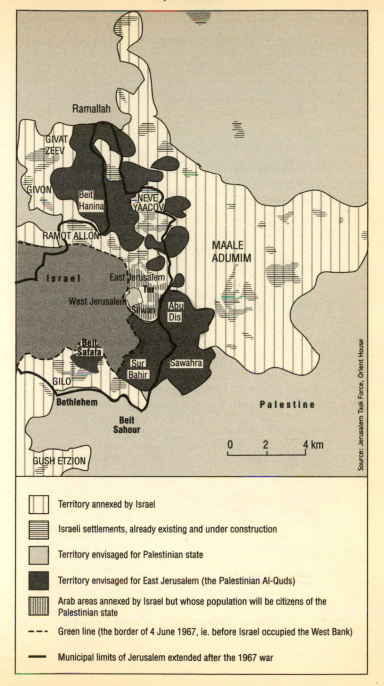

Israel's Camp David II Proposals for a Palestinian State

Source: Jerusalem Task Force, Orient House

Israeli settlements, existing or under construction

	Palestinian state suggested by Israel
	Zones A and B under partial control of the Palestinian Authority
	Palestinian localities to be annexed by Israel
	Palestinian territory to be annexed by Israel
	Projected Israeli Security Zone
	Roads serving Israeli settlements
	Green line (borders at 4 June 1967)
	Israeli settlements, existing or under construction

0   10 km

Israel's Camp David II Proposals for a Palestinian State

ACKNOWLEDGEMENTS

This book was made possible thanks to the efforts and support of a number of colleagues and friends. Comments and insights by Alain Joxe and Saida Bedar of Le Centre Interdisciplinaire de Recherches sur la Paix et des Etudes Stratégiques (CIRPES) in Paris were indispensable in sharpening the focus and the analysis, and covering the necessary ground. My friend and research assistant Nabih Bashir, who researched the documents at the Hebrew University, insured the needed efficacity and resourcefulness. Updates and research support from the Center for Policy Analysis on Palestine, Washington, and particularly the encouragement of Hisham Sharabi and Heidi Shoup, made the work a worthwhile challenge. My thanks are due also to Salpy Eskidjian and Dwain Ebbs of the World Council of Churches. The list could go on much more, and includes Cecilia Joxe, François Geze, Beatrice Cazer, Hall Gardner, Alain Gresh, Farida Salfiti, Khader Shkeirat, Amnon Raz, Muhammad Hassanein Heykal, my dear brother Azmi Bishara and many others.

The encouragement of Anne Rodford, Robert Molteno and other members of Zed Books made updating this book possible. Richard Falk has been kind to cooperate and correspondence with him made the work a constant intellectual challenge.

Special thanks go to my students at the American University of Paris, whose enthusiasm, curiosity and matter-of-factness helped clarify and simplify the work. Updating the book in the spring of 2002 was not easy while so many civilians were being killed, wounded and imprisoned, but was nonetheless inspired by those Palestinians and Israelis who yearn for liberty and justice.

FOREWORD

RICHARD FALK

Never have the prospects for peace between Israel and Palestine seemed worse, and never has the quest for peace seemed more vital as both a moral and political imperative. It is a moral imperative to emancipate both peoples from the daily ordeal of terrorist tactics, as well as to liberate the Palestinians as a captive people after decades of oppression and severe deprivation. It is a political imperative because the Israeli/Palestinian violence can at any point spiral out of control, engulfing the region in bitter turmoil and severe civil strife, if not regional war on a large scale that might persist for years.

And yet despite these obvious pressures to find a solution, the odds seem stacked against rationality as well as against morality. The United States Government has linked its response to the September 11 attacks with a campaign against all forms of anti-state political violence, effectively mandating states everywhere to step up their violence against oppositional movements and self-determination struggles. No leader has taken this cue more avidly than Ariel Sharon, audaciously proclaiming that Yasser Arafat was Israel's 'Osama Bin Laden.' As a result, Israeli maximalist goals of continued domination of the Palestinian territories seem attainable.

True, there are some slender rays of hope that penetrate the dark clouds that hover above the blood-soaked holy land. Europe seems, at last, more willing to be active and balanced, providing credibility as an intermediary diplomatic force that is growing visibly impatient with Washington's partisanship. And even the US Government, at least in the State Department, seems to recognize that re-starting the peace process for Israel/Palestine is an essential precondition both for regional stability in the Middle East and to obtain support in the Islamic world for the main US undertaking directed against the al-Qaida network, with its cells of extremists distributed in many countries. Also encouraging is Colin Powell's initiative to convene later in 2002 a ministerial meeting on the Israel/Palestine conflict under the joint auspices of 'the Quartet': United States, Russia, the European Union, and the United Nations. Bringing these actors into a responsible diplomatic role offers the parties a credible framework if the political will exists on the part of Israeli and Palestinian leaders.

But still, it is hard to be hopeful given the variety of facts on the ground, the rising influence of extremists on both sides, and the domestic pro-Israeli bias in the United States, especially in the US Congress. There is still little understanding of just how desperate the situation really is for ordinary Palestinians, continuously oppressed, harassed, intimidated, and increasingly pushed below the poverty line, and, at the same time, taking note of yet more Israeli settlements (34 authorized in the year that Sharon has been Prime Minister) and of additional Israeli efforts to create sealed 'cantons' on the West Bank that make travel and mobility even within occupied Palestine a daily ordeal.

Against such a background the appearance of a new edition of Marwan Bishara's *Palestine/Israel: Peace or Apartheid* is timely, providing a text that comes as close to being required reading as anything currently available, giving both information and an informed, accurate, and realistic account of the failures of past efforts to establish peace. Bishara's analysis of the failure of the Oslo peace process is particularly devastating, warning us all to oppose its resumption, which has seemed to be the recommendation of many influential voices, including that of the Mitchell Commission. The book is invaluable also in showing the horrifying consequences of settling for the status quo of occupation and settlement, with its apartheid implications, and the inevitable resonance such realities have with the criminally racist regime that long ruled the black majority in South Africa.

Bishara pins his hopes on the possibility that, stepping center stage from the wings of Israeli power, will come an Israeli de Gaulle, or at least an Israeli de Klerk, who has the prestige, stature, and courage to break the Gordian Knot of occupation, withdraw definitively, dismantle the settlements, address the refugee issue humanely, and share Jerusalem and water equitably. Of course, such an expectation, as Bishara knows better than the rest of us, is a longshot, possibly even a case of waiting for Godot. But to understand that without some dramatic sort of rupture, the dreadful existing situation will persist, and worsen, validating the darkest forebodings on both sides, is to convey the grim circumstances with which the search for peace must contend.

As Bishara clearly portrays, from a historical perspective, Palestine has already given Israel extraordinary concessions that are not generally appreciated as bearing on the contours of what now would be a fair solution at this point. The Palestinian Authority has conceded pre-1967 Israel as a Jewish state, which comprises about 78% of historic Palestine, leaving for negotiations the remaining 22% to satisfy the aspirations of a Palestinian population that is at least equal, and possibly considerably larger than the Jewish population of Israel. To ask Palestinians to compromise their sovereign rights over this 22%, including the acceptance of settlements and settlers, must be understood in this light. And secondly, and as significantly, the Palestinians seek peace within the Zionist template of ethnic states, which runs counter to the modern notions of statehood that had regarded only secular, multi-national states as fully legitimate. Such a concession defeats the Palestinian preference for a normal state of their own, and consigns the large Palestinian minority in Israel (about 1.2 million) to a permanent condition of openly second-class citizenship. To find a solution that will be acceptable to the Palestinians, it is necessary to take serious account of these two sets of limiting conditions.

Bishara is very keenly aware that international law is on the side of the Palestinians with respect to every major issue in contention: withdrawal from the territories occupied in 1967, right of return of Palestinian refugees expelled or departed in 1948, sovereignty over Jerusalem, status of the settlements, both throughout the territories and within the expanded jurisdiction of Jerusalem. This assessment of Palestinian rights is a matter of a consensus among members of the United Nations, including such expert bodies as the Human Rights Commission, and among international law experts who are not closely tied to Israeli or American policy perspectives.

One of the notable features of the Oslo Peace Process that has been given little attention is the exclusion of the relevance of these international law considerations from negotiations. Every attempt to challenge feverish Israeli settlement expansion during the 1990s was ruled out of order by Washington and Israel as interfering with the peace process, in which context the issue of settlements was among those matters that would be addressed when the parties got around to 'final status negotiations.' But the effect of such an indulgence of illegality was to generate 'facts on the ground,' as well as to send mixed messages to moderate Palestinians. Why were Israelis invested so heavily in the settlements and an elaborate network of bypass roads if they were willing to give the Palestinians a viable state that would satisfy Palestinian rights of self-determination? Such a question has still not received a satisfactory answer.

If we suggest that this international law support of basic Palestinian demands relates to 'inalienable Palestinian rights', what should be the consequence? In a perfect world, such rights would be fully respected, but to insist here on such a framework for peace would probably end what little prospects exist for agreeing on a fair solution. At the very least, the starting point will have to abandon claims arising from territorial injustices prior to 1967, basing the search for a fair solution on the proposition that the Palestinian state would be an ethnic state on the 22% of the original Palestine. But within that 22% there are strong reasons of justice and practicality to demand that future diplomatic efforts, unlike Oslo, take account of international law from Day One, including Israeli obligations to respect the Fourth Geneva Convention governing military occupation. As a practical matter it would mean renouncing the settlements, respecting the rights of the Palestinian civilian population, abandoning the alteration of the geographical boundaries and demographic composition of Jerusalem to maximize the Israeli presence in the city, and opening up negotiations on the past and present rights of Palestinian refugees.

Only such a commitment to this kind of fairness can hope to produce 'peace' for both peoples. There are risks to Israel from pursuing such a path, and one never knows fully how successful the assured efforts of extremists on both sides to wreck a genuine peace process will become. It is well to remember that de Gaulle's effort to end the Algerian War brought France to the brink of civil war. Reversing course is never easy, nor is success assured. But what of the alternatives? As Bishara so powerfully demonstrates, 'apartheid' for the Palestinians, and 'terrorism' for the Israelis. With such a destiny lying in wait, surely taking risks for peace should be the prayer and commitment of every person on both sides of the green line, as well as people elsewhere who care about peace and justice for both Palestinians and Israelis, and seek to revive Jerusalem as a prime site of holy pilgrimage for the three monotheistic peoples, as well as for the spiritually inclined throughout the world.

Richard Falk
Santa Barbara, California

PROLOGUE

BUSH HOLDS PALESTINE
HOSTAGE TO SHARON

The American plan for resolving the Israel-Palestine conflict revealed in late June 2002 has condemned Palestinians and Israelis to another chapter of bloodshed. The Bush administration has repeated the mistakes of the past instead of charting a truly new vision for the future.

At Israel's behest, Bush chose to ignore two important briefing papers lying on his desk - one describing a comprehensive Arab initiative that charts a peaceful future free of occupation, the other from Yasser Arafat, the only elected Palestinian leader, accepting as a framework for future negotiations the ideas put forward by President Bill Clinton in December 2000.

Like many before him, Bush feels inclined to think up a 'creative' way out of an easily soluble problem. The end result is a formula to manage the crisis rather one that resolves it. Sadly, the solution to this conflict - Israel's complete withdrawal from the territories it occupied in 1967 in exchange for peace with its Arab neighbors, or 'land for peace' - has been known for decades. It has also been ignored for decades.

Bush wants us to return to an interim process, but with a new Palestinian leadership. A smart US policy, I learned from my Washington visits, is a safe policy - one that avoids dealing with Israel's Ariel Sharon by dumping on the Palestinians. Bush, having learned from his father's experience, knows all about the consequences of pressuring Israel. While claiming that Yasser

Arafat cannot be trusted, the American president has proved that
he cannot be trusted with the Middle East.

Bush demands a change of Palestinian leadership to pave the
way toward a Palestinian state at some point in the future. But
in a democracy, the leadership is the choice of the people. Until
another president is elected in free and open elections, no one
has the right to impose a leader on the Palestinians. With Israeli
tanks occupying all the Palestinian territories, and many of the
leaders in Israeli and Palestinian jails or in hiding, it's hard to
see how free and open elections could be held.

The second-best scenario is for Arafat to name the most popular leader in Palestine today as his deputy and possible future
leader, and have him negotiate with Israel. Marwan Barghouti,
an elected legislator and able politician, is well versed in Israeli
politics and speaks Hebrew fluently. Although he is in an Israeli
prison, it would not be the first time that a national leader, as
was the case with Nelson Mandela, was able to arrive at a peace
deal with his captors.

Bush told us that the interim period would take three years.
The incremental approach was designed to build trust between
the parties. Peace is a process, we were told. Yet, rather than
addressing the problem - Israel's brutal 35-year occupation of
Palestinian lands - the incremental process will lead to more
Israeli domination and more illegal settlements rather than to a
peace settlement.

Why is Bush building another tunnel in order to see the light?
Ultimately this new plan will absolve his administration of any
serious commitment or decisions that might conflict with Israel.
When the 'permanent' solution comes up on the agenda of the
next administration, the strategic map of the region will have
been altered, probably for the worse. Bush's 'Axis of Evil' policy is already threatening another escalation against Iraq, Iran
and other countries.

Meanwhile, adding three years of uncertainty to the Oslo
peace process's seven years of ambiguity means more process

and less peace. This will once more enable Israeli leaders to evade the choice that Israel will eventually have to make: Does it want land or does it want peace? Peace and occupation are as incompatible as right and wrong.

Instead of addressing this incompatibility, the United States seems content to bury its head in the sand in the mistaken belief that if the Palestinians hear the word 'state' they will roll over and this conflict will be over. But a state cannot be the alternative to a fair solution, it must be the culmination of sound policies that lead to the end of occupation.

As the region descends into an abyss of destructive Palestinian suicide and Israeli homicide, one is left with two options in treating the cancer of the occupation and the resulting conflict. The first option, a pharmaceutical one, entails more prescriptions to ease the pain and lower the temperature in the hope that the cancer will go away. The second, surgical solution takes on the proliferating causes of the conflict, namely the illegal settlements. This entails the uncompromising implementation of international law, which rules inadmissible the holding and settlement of territory by force. The alternative, the feeding of Israel's culture of impunity, can only nurture the Palestinian culture of suicide bombings.

Meanwhile, Middle East witch doctors are proliferating in Israel and Palestine, producing more religious fundamentalism and more irrationality. If the only earthly laws that apply in their land are those of the jungle - rule by brute force - then both sides will become more inclined to apply religious interpretations and laws. A religious and communitarian conflict would have grave consequences for both peoples for a long time to come.

But judging from Bush's end-quote from the bible, one is still left with the fear that the dangerous and fanatical politics of the Christian Right at home are being exported abroad through the republican foreign policy. In fact, by June 2002, the support in the Republican party for Israel was four times higher than that in the Democratic party where Jewish influence has been evident for decades.

Half a century ago, America began to see the Israel-Palestine conflict in the context of the Cold War; today the Bush administration is putting the same unresolved conflict in the framework of its crusade against terrorism and evil. The new geotheology of the American Right is further complicating a precarious situation of elementary colonialism in the Holy Land. Unless rational voices in the Middle East, Europe, the US and elsewhere make themselves heard, the suffering of the people of the region will continue unabated. The silence today regarding the Palestinians is but a reminder of the silence in the last century regarding the Jews.

INTRODUCTION

Despite the continuing violence, the Israeli and Palestinian delegations to the peace negotiations in Paris in May 2001 reached a framework agreement on ending the century-old conflict. American and United Nations delegates heard an impassioned plea from 'Dina', head of the Palestinian delegation, on the need for Palestinian self-determination in a sovereign state, and were treated to a clear-headed proposal from 'Emily', the Israeli delegate, on security concerns and future cooperation. Following some sleepless nights, the two sides agreed on several guiding principles. Jerusalem would be an open city and the capital of two states, with Israeli sovereignty in West Jerusalem and Palestinian sovereignty in East Jerusalem. Free trade, open borders, and complementary economic policies were underlined as ways of fostering confidence and cooperation. The parents of some of the delegates were unhappy with the results, even accusing their children of betrayal, but the students themselves felt that their achievement was something to be celebrated.

Perhaps it is facile to place importance on the success of these simulated negotiations held by students at the American University of Paris, where I teach. However, it is significant that a deal was reached simply because the students realized that any deal must be based on justice. These students were confronted with the same dilemma that haunts Israelis and Palestinians 53 years after the founding of Israel. What can be prescribed for the 4.5 million Jews and almost 4.5 million Palestinians fighting over the land of Palestine/Israel, given that in the 21st century neither colonialism nor a form of apartheid are credible options? Separation of the two peoples in two sovereign and viable states was the immediate answer of our delegates. The Israeli side in our simulated negotiations recognized 95 percent of the West Bank and all of Gaza as Palestinian territory and acknowledged the Right of Return for Palestinian refugees. Both sides agreed that, though the refugees would return primarily to the Palestinian state, the first 350,000 could return to Israel over a five-year period. Further negotiations would then ensue. The Palestinian delegation accepted Israel's annexation of four blocs of settlements on the Green Line in return for comparable land around Gaza, while Israel agreed to evacuate the rest of the settlements.

This was not a far-fetched compromise. In reality, however, the Middle East is anything but a case study of the application of international standards. Times are tough for an educator, especially when it comes to teaching on the use of force or conflict resolution, as I have been doing. The Middle East is an academic Pandora's box of diplomatic flops, violations of international law, and illegal occupation and terrorism. Israel has written the new manual on how to violate international law and compromise universal values. In response, more Palestinians seem to have given up on the international community and international law - the most potent weapon of the weak - adopting instead the drastic method of suicide attacks.

As our simulation excercise was drawing to a close in May 2001, the international American-led Mitchell Commission, after five months of investigating the roots of the ongoing violence, called on April 30 for a ceasefire and an immediate freeze on Israeli settlements, considering them to be the main cause of the escalation of violence. The Palestinian leader, Yasser Arafat, accepted the Mitchell recommendation in order to stop the escalation, as did most Israelis, according to independent Israeli polls, but not Israeli leaders who have repeatedly rejected any halt to settlement activity. Indeed, Israeli Prime Minister Ariel Sharon actually proposed $400 million for further expansion and, within a year, he had built 40 new settlement posts (*Newsweek*, May 23, 2002). Absent from my class, Israel's leader missed the basic lesson that war in Palestine, contrary to the Clausewitz doctrine, is not diplomacy by other means. With the triumph of Mr. Sharon's logic in the Occupied Territories, the Israeli-Palestinian dilemma has entered a dangerous new era - an era of Apartheid, in which many more people will die in vain and separation into two independent states becomes diminishingly attractive in what was Mandate Palestine.

THE LEGACY OF OSLO

In this context, it is all the more important to break away from the dramatic images of children confronting tanks and the bloody scenes of suicide bombings in order to understand the factors behind the escalation of the conflict. This book analyses how the seven-year peace process, begun with the Oslo agreement, handled the problem of the occupation in both its political and historical dimensions. Learning from the failure of the Oslo process is particularly important not only in order to understand the present impasse, but also to avoid repeating the same mistakes. This is easy to do theoretically in class, but in the Middle East the lesson is lost on people and politicians as they play the blame game. Since the failure of the Oslo process, at least ten Israeli/Palestinian peace initiatives or plans have been put forward. Almost all have repeated the mistakes of the past: partial steps, open-ended negotiations in stages, and implementation in phases, leaving the goal at the mercy of destructive ambiguity while accepting continuous violations of signed agreements and international law in the absence of a potent implementation mechanism.

The Oslo process must, first and foremost, be understood in its historic and geo-strategic contexts. It came about only after a series of fruitless Israeli attempts to defuse the Palestine question without resolving it. Four decades of ethnic cleansing, massacres, and wars failed to have the desired effect for Israel. The first Intifada of 1987, like the Soweto uprising in South Africa's townships a decade earlier, came as a rude awakening to the world that racism could not go on indefinitely. The uprising persisted for six years, in spite of officially sanctioned brutality, and was able to disrupt the daily life of occupation. It was only after those 6 years that Israel utilized the window of opportunity that presented itself with the end of the Cold War and the defeat of Iraq, coupled with a divided Arab world, in order to reach a deal with the Palestinians. With Washington's help, it physically and demographically divided up the West Bank and Gaza into islands of poverty, or bantustans, while maintaining economic domination and direct control over Palestinian land and natural resources.

This self-serving Israeli maneuver was referred to as 'the peace process'. It turned out to be Apartheid. Oslo was based on a balance of power, not on international legality and fairness. After years of rejecting the interventions of the international community or any notion of an international conference to settle this question, Israel convinced a politically and financially bankrupt Palestine Liberation Organization (PLO) to engage in a direct bilateral relation in Oslo where Israel would have the upper hand. Indeed, the imbalance between the weak and occupied Palestinians face-to-face with American-supported Israel was the primary cause of the failure of their bilateral agreements. What Israel considered a dream come true in Oslo, turned into the Palestinians' nightmare under Israeli dictates. Instead of being a fair arbitrator in the talks by making up for the imbalance of power, the Clinton administration supported its strategic ally, Israel, on all issues, while blocking or marginalizing the role of the international community.

In revising this book, I shall begin with a quick balance sheet of the dramatic events of last year, from mid-2001, especially the trickle-down effect of Sharon's election and the bombings of the World Trade Center and the Pentagon that led to changed priorities in America and to Israel's cynical use of the 'War on Terrorism' to break the Palestinian Authority (PA) and undo the Oslo process.

THE DEMISE OF THE OSLO PROCESS

The collapse of the Oslo process began when the Israeli government and the Palestinians realized they could not attain their goals through diplomacy. The Palestinians perceived Oslo as a de-colonialization process that, following the historical pattern, should lead to self-determination and an independent state alongside Israel in the territories occupied in 1967. For its part, Israel utilized the process to transform its direct military control into indirect domination over the Palestinians by reserving for itself the right to determine the nature and borders of the Palestinian entity within the constraints of the security imperatives of its own illegal settlements. When the diplomatic process failed to produce the desired results, the then Israeli Prime Minister, Ehud Barak, used the military to restore 'order', eliminate Palestinian gains by crushing the Intifada, and break the will of those who poured into the streets demanding their freedom from occupation and their right to independence.

The Mitchell report, a 'must-read', concluded that there was no evidence to Israeli claims that the PA instigated the Intifada. In fact, the American-led international commission described the Intifada as a series of confrontations between mostly unarmed Palestinians and heavily armed Israeli security whose excessive and disproportionate use of force led to 60 Palestinians killed and a thousand injured, in comparison to five dead Israelis. Barak knew the outcome if the Palestinians did not accept his humiliating dictates. He said that unless a full agreement was reached, there would be a full-scale confrontation. This politically criminal approach led directly to the escalation. Israel's response was typical, reckoning that military force was a safer bet than the alternative of political channels.

When force failed to achieve the necessary objectives, Israel applied more force. Unfortunately, Israel's inability to translate its military victories into political gains through a peace agreement led to the present deterioration of its security. Each successive Israeli leader did their bit in trampling on the peace process: Shamir stalled it, Rabin militarized it, Netanyahu undermined it, and Barak outdid it. Not a single one of these Israeli leaders finished his term from the outset of the peace process because they could not make peace while maintaining the occupation and settlements. Yitzhak Rabin and Shimon Peres promised peace. The first was assassinated and the second was voted out. Binyamin Netanyahu and Ehud Barak promised 'peace and security', and were also voted out.

In spite of all this, Washington remained adamant that its peace process was the only game in sight. The escalation was contained and, against all odds, the Oslo process seemed to survive the deterioration. Washington was particularly anxious to maintain a diplomatic framework for its post-Gulf War policy in the Middle East until a new Pax-Americana was set in motion. In order to achieve calm and a return to the negotiating table, special American envoy, CIA Director George Tenet, came out with his own plan to implement the Mitchell recommendations. In the process, he de-politicized Mitchell by reducing the status of Palestinians and Israelis from two political entities to two security bodies. When that failed, the Bush administration sent retired General Anthony Zinni, who offered his approach, making Palestinian security subservient once more to Israeli security, hence departing completely from the international Mitchell Commission. With the failure to reinvigorate the peace process at Taba over the following few months, especially after Barak pulled out from the negotiations at the Egyptian resort, Sharon's victory was assured and the end of the process was all but announced.

THE ADVENT OF SHARON

Sharon's election in February 2001 signaled the beginning of the end of the peace process. Within a year, he turned back the clock on efforts to reach a historic reconciliation between Israelis and Palestinians and underlined the inescapable fact that Israel, not Palestine, was the source of instability and conflict in the region.

Shaken and disillusioned, a colonial Israel had offered its electors two generals, one (Sharon) notorious for his war crimes since the 1950s, and another (Barak) an arrogant soldier with more than one chip on his shoulder, who had been responsible for bombing Palestinian towns with F-16s and Apache helicopters. The Israelis chose, in the words of then acting Foreign Minister Shlomo Ben Ami, a new Israeli Milosevic. Indeed, under international law, Sharon's bloody record merits his indictment for crimes against humanity, including the systematic and willful killing of civilians during war. To the Israelis, once Barak had declared that Israel had no peace partner after Camp David, General Sharon appeared to be a fitting alternative. Contrary to American claims that it was Arafat's actions that had led to Sharon's election, the latter's electoral victory came essentially as a culmination of the failure of the Israeli government to exploit the window of opportunity presented at Oslo, and the three decades of radicalisation within Israeli society since its occupation of the West Bank and Gaza in 1967.

Israel has slowly but consistently moved to the Right under the influence of radical nationalist and religious fanatics who ruled it for a quarter of a century. The only exception was the ill-fated period of the Rabin/Peres governments, made possible only after then Secretary of State James Baker threatened Israel with economic sanctions in 1991.

Barak, when his turn came, could hardly be seen as moderate and the Knesset was more radical during his tenure than its predecessors. In spite of Sharon's declared war-platform and his long, bloody record, Israel's friends in the West went on promoting the possibility of a Sharon peace - a contradiction in terms. This proved to be not only wishful thinking, but awfully dangerous. Unrelenting, America's marketing of a transformed Sharon, relative to the populist Netanyahu, or other radicals in government, as one who could effect withdrawal from the occupied Palestinian land, has been cynically misleading. Sharon reckons illegal Israeli settlements and peace are not incompatible. He actually told his American counterparts that settlements are good for peace.

In reality, Sharon's war on peace has been a crusade to protect

the expansion of Israeli settlers in the Occupied Territories, leaving
all Israelis under an even worse security threat. He has made it clear
that, only after bludgeoning the Palestinians into submission would
he sign an agreement with them. He seeks the peace of the dead.
During the worst Israeli escalation against the Palestinians,
President Bush, with a straight face, told journalists in the White
House that Sharon was a 'man of peace'. Sharon's delaying tactics
to disrupt a return to the negotiating table were his only diplomatic
contribution. His 'numerical doctrine', according to *Haaretz's*
leading diplomatic correspondent, Aluf Ben, meant that: First came
the seven days quiet that he demanded of the Palestinians. Then
there were the six demands made of Syria and the five fundamentals
of the '100 percent effort' against terrorism, not to mention the four
essentials for reform in the Palestinian Authority, the two
conditions for beginning diplomatic negotiations and the one prime
minister who wants to stay in power. And when you add it all up,
you arrive at a result of zero diplomatic progress (*Haaretz*, May 23,
2002).

In the process, Sharon slammed the door on a landmark Arab
initiative that offered Israel regional guarantees for its well-being
in the Middle East within secure and recognized borders, in return
for its withdrawal from the Occupied Territories. The Arab summit
that convened in Beirut unanimously adopted a Saudi initiative that
envisioned a one-time deal of total withdrawal for total peace. It
reiterated the international consensus, namely implementing UN
Security Resolution 242, considered the basis of the peace process.
Three-fifths of the Israeli public and most of the world supported
the Arab initiative, if that could bring peace, but not Sharon. He
rejects the notion of Israeli withdrawal and refuses to dismantle a
single settlement. Worse, he responded to the Arab initiative by
ordering the invasion of the autonomous Palestinian territories and
blockading Yasser Arafat's headquarters. This was déjà vu all over
again.

Two decades earlier, in 1981, Saudi King Fahd had proposed a
peace initiative, later adopted by the Arab summit in Fez, Morocco

in 1982, that sent out peace overtures to end the conflict. In response, and in line with Arab overtures, then US President Ronald Reagan came out with his own plan that included a freeze on the settlements. The Begin/Sharon government rejected all overtures out of hand and warned Washington not to coordinate with the Saudis. In 1982 Begin gave Sharon the green light to invade Lebanon in pursuit of the PLO. Arafat was incarcerated and Beirut bombed.

This time around, however - twenty years later - President George W. Bush's administration learned from the mistakes of its predecessors and played with a 'vision' of a provisional Palestinian state, then promptly negated it by putting that vision into the hands of Sharon.

In addition to rejecting the Reagan Plan, Israel rejected the 1969 American Rogers Plan, the 1977 Carter ideas, the 1988 Shultz Plan, and the Baker ideas of 1991. According to Robert Malley, a Clinton advisor on the peace process, Barak also rejected Clinton's ideas repeatedly at Camp David and afterwards. Israel, to borrow a phrase in a different context from Abba Eban, did not miss an opportunity to miss an opportunity that could enable it to live in peace in the Middle East. Sharon portrayed his war and invasion of the autonomous territories as an extension of Israel's 1948 war of independence. This is a flagrant manipulation of Israeli insecurity; it has clearly been a war of choice, not so different from Sharon's 1982 invasion of Lebanon. As he had promised, Sharon went on to undo years of process and ruined a decade of Palestinian institution building. He tried to achieve what his mentor Yitzhak Shamir had insisted on: security without peace. In the space of a single year, Sharon reversed all that had been agreed upon between Israelis and Palestinians and destroyed much of the international community's economic and political investments in Palestine.

2002: DESTRUCTION WREAKS HAVOC

By the Spring of 2002, the Israeli military had wreaked its wrath on dozens of Palestinian towns, camps, and villages, reaching a new record in Palestine. From Hebron to Jenin through Ramallah and Bethlehem, military vandalism and destruction were witnessed everywhere. The media coverage of the Intifada and Israeli invasion confined itself to images of Israeli and Palestinian casualties. By late June, the casualties since September 2000 had climbed to over 1,650 Palestinians and 550 Israelis dead, in addition to tens of thousands injured, the majority being Palestinians, many crippled for life.

While Israel emphasized that there was no genocide in Palestine, ignoring the military's wonton destruction of the Palestinian Authority's very infrastructure, its crimes in the occupied Palestinian land constituted 'politi-cide' - paralysing Palestinian institutional political life through assassination, imprisonment, incarceration of the Palestinians' elected leaders, and vandalism of ministries and other official buildings. During its invasion, Israel arrested thousands of Palestinians and assassinated dozens of leaders - mostly from the secular Fatah faction, whose leader, Marwan Barghuti, was one of those arrested. One of the most popular politicians in Palestine, Barghuti is an elected member of the Palestinian Legislative Council and is committed to coexistence with Israel. He has been tortured and interrogated after enforced sleep deprivation.

Israel is also responsible for the total destruction of the Palestinian economy (what I may call 'econo-cide'), the ruin of Palestinian urban centres (urbani-cide) and the defacing of the Palestinian landscape with settlements and the bypass roads for the settlers connecting them. According to the *New York Times*, 'It's safe to say that the infrastructure of life itself and of any future Palestinian state - roads, schools, electricity, pylons, water pipes, telephone lines - has been devastated.' (*New York Times*, April 10, 2002).

In the space of a year, Israeli Prime Minister Sharon had destroyed all that was left of the Oslo process by bombardment from the air and the ground, having blockaded Palestinian towns and villages for months. The Palestinian economic infrastructure was now in ruins, with collateral damage of several billion dollars, and the Israelis gripped by the fear of suicide bombs. Sharon's 2002 March invasion cost about half a billion dollars, and eight times that amount once the effect on the Palestinian economy was factored in. In a May 2002 speech in the Norwegian capital, Terje Larsen, one of the Oslo architects, stated: 'The Oslo process has collapsed; the institutions it created have been destroyed.'

Israel's policy led to a one-third contraction of the Palestinian gross national product (GNP) from September 2000 to the end of 2001 - or $1.5 billion annually. In a matter of a few weeks in the Spring of 2002, a further half billion dollars of physical property losses and additional hundreds of millions of dollars of losses in the Palestinian gross domestic product (GDP) were caused by Sharon's invasion of the autonomous territories. All of this was in addition to a 25 percent reduction in the GDP over the course of the seven years of the peace process. Israeli soldiers broke into most official and informational offices - including the Bureau of Statistics, universities and other institutions relating to state building in Palestine - and stole the hard disks of their computer systems.

However, this should have come as no surprise. More than two decades ago, Palestinian historian Walid Khalidi concluded an article in *Foreign Affairs* (1978) by stating that the real security question for a Palestinian state is: 'how long would the [Israeli] brigadier generals be able to keep their hands off such a delectable sitting duck?' Sharon's answer: not long. Jenin's refugee camp in northern Palestine, home to some 12,000 Palestinian refugees, is a good example of the new Israeli chutzpah. During the invasion of the camp, the army carried out war crimes against civilians as it razed and destroyed hundreds of homes, and killed and injured hundreds more Palestinians, often leaving them to bleed to death. A few days later, the same Israeli forces returned to the camp bringing on it more destruction in order to prove that its aggression was unstoppable, regardless of UN Security Council resolutions condemning the invasion. Sharon refused to allow a special UN team of experts to look into the events in the camp where human rights organizations testified to the committing of war crimes.

The same happened in Bethlehem. Only a few days after Israel had lifted its blockade on the Church of the Nativity, it re-entered the city and installed its soldiers near the holy site. Other Palestinian towns and camps faced similar destruction and vandalism and repeated bloody incursions.

CLOSURE OF THE WEST BANK AND ISRAELI SECURITY

After its brutal invasion and tornado-like destruction of the autonomous areas, the Israeli army in May 2002 closed off all of the West Bank and paved the way for a new order. This new order was based on occupation in the West Bank and a higher economic and social price tag for Palestinian society. Israel banned all Palestinian travel between towns without a special permit issued by the Israeli military command centre in the West Bank settlements. Movement of Palestinians to Israel and East Jerusalem was prohibited. The movement of goods between Palestinian cities within the West Bank, as well as from Israel to the West Bank, was subjected to a 'back-to- back' system whereby goods need to be offloaded from the incoming trucks and then reloaded onto local trucks.

A total of eight locations to enforce the post-invasion system marked another partition of the autonomous territories into eight separate bantustans. Movement into Gaza was allowed only for humanitarian goods, and materials for donor-funded projects were allowed in on a case-by-case basis and coordinated in advance. The Israeli army violated international law, especially the Fourth Geneva Convention, as well as the Oslo-defined borders between the autonomous Palestinian areas and Israel, making them contingent on the movement of Israeli tanks. It unilaterally transformed Israel's presumed temporary encirclement of the Palestinians into a permanent bantustanization of these urban centers with so-called security zones, instituting barbed wire fences, a permit system, and pass regulations for the circulation of Palestinian goods and people. Israeli incursions into Palestinian areas under the guise of fighting terrorism were made at the behest of Israeli military commanders and leaders, and became an Israeli prerogative. Israeli measures undermined international aid and Palestinian attempts to piece back together their shattered lives and reform their institutions in the autonomous territories.

As was to be expected, Israel's de facto Apartheid system in the occupied West Bank and Gaza only engendered further violence. From the outset, these measures brought about large-scale downsizing or even total cessation of production and raised unemployment - already over 50 percent in the towns and over 70 percent in the camps - and increased poverty - already above 50 percent, with most families living on as little as $2 dollars a day. According to the International Monetary Fund (IMF) and the World Bank, closures had the most devastating effect on the Palestinian economy. Arafat fattened his bureaucracy by 120,000 salaries in order to reduce the unemployment caused by closures. The closures hampered economic competition and strengthened the monopolies of Arafat's cronies over basic products. Further economic decline led to increased despair and radicalisation within Palestinian society, in the same way that the effective functioning of the Palestinian security forces was limited by the destruction of their buildings and prisons.

REFORM AND OCCUPATION

While ignoring the burning issue of the occupation, the American-led international community shied away from recognizing Israeli crimes in the Palestinian territories and instead focused on the necessity for the political and security reform of Palestinian self-rule as a way out of the impasse.

Needless to say, Palestinians see reform differently from Americans and Israelis. Palestinian society is hoping for reform that can bring it freedom and accountable government, that can improve access to employment, education and health, while the Israeli-driven American approach foresees a security and political reform that prioritizes Israeli settlements and interests in occupied Palestine. The badly needed improvement in Palestinian living conditions has become impossible under Sharon's bantustans plan. As long as Israel brands all Palestinian political parties as terrorist, the establishment of a political process in Palestine is a farce. Palestinian political leaders have either been assassinated or imprisoned by Israel and the PA. Many are on the run, hiding for their safety.

Convening elections under such circumstances would be a mockery of the democratic process. Moreover, introducing a constitution, independent judiciary, or other democratic institutions recommended by international commissions and Palestinian civil society activists, can hardly occur in the absence of a functioning Legislative Council. For two years Israel has banned legislators from convening, while targeting and imprisoning council members. Ironically, Sharon made negotiations contingent on effecting 'Palestinian reform', while his military made sure that no political or economic reform could be implemented under a state of siege. In truth, by reform, Sharon's government meant reforming the security services into more responsive and better organized bodies to carry out Israel's bidding in the Occupied Territories. Israelis have long encouraged or facilitated corruption and nepotism among Palestinian officials and businessmen, or simply looked the other way as Israeli businessmen and ex-security officials worked out shadowy deals with their Palestinian counterparts. This gave those Palestinian VIPs the incentive to further collaborate with Israel and look the other way as Israel expanded its domination and settlement activity in the territories.

Sharon's attempt to deflect international pressure went hand-in-hand with discrediting the Palestinian National Authority (PNA) and demonizing its elected leader, Arafat. In the words of Oxford Israeli historian Avi Shlaim:

> In fact, the PA consists of a group of moderate members who joined Arafat in renouncing terror and in opting for the political path to progress. It is a government in the making, with an annual budget

of a billion dollars, charged with providing essential services to the 3,300,000 inhabitants of the territories. Among its 150,000 employees are not just policemen and security men, but civil servants, schoolteachers, welfare officers, doctors, and hospital workers. About 1,000,000 Palestinians depend for their livelihood on wages paid by the PA. Dismantling the PA would lead to chaos, instability, and endemic violence. This would not serve the interests of Israeli security, but it may provide the pretext that Sharon is looking for to reoccupy the West Bank, to continue the process of creeping annexation, and to 'transfer' some of its inhabitants to the neighboring Arab countries. (April 4, 2002)

Indeed, the real intention behind Sharon's influential security cabinet of settlers, religious fundamentalists, and diehard generals is to undo past peace processes and deter future peace initiatives that might hamper the expansion of the illegal settlements in the Palestinian territories.

FROM DREAM TO NIGHTMARE

If someone had told the Jews who formed 10 percent of Palestine's population at the turn of the last century that one day they would have a state spreading over 78 percent of the country with 80 percent of Jerusalem as its capital, they would have dismissed this as no more than a beautiful dream. If the other 90 percent of Palestine's population were told that one day they would give up three-quarters of their land, after three-quarters of their population had become refugees, and that they would be forced to live in 10-18 percent of their homeland, perforated like a Swiss cheese by 200 illegal settlements protected by a nuclear-armed neighbour run by an infamous general, they would have thought they were being offered a nightmare. When the nightmare became a reality, more and more Palestinians were willing, like the biblical Samson, to bring down the temple on the Israelis and themselves. After Israel, under Barak, responded to stone-throwing and sporadic

sniping by terrorizing Palestinian cities with F-16 warplanes and
Apache helicopter gunships, Palestinians resorted to suicide
bombings against Israeli civilians.

Make no mistake, Israel has always dictated the level of violence
in Palestine. Eventually the utter failure of the peace process to
deliver security, liberty, and dignity left the Palestinians at the mercy
of Israeli might. The impotence of the international community in
light of American identification with Israel, European indifference,
and Arab disunity drove the Palestinians to their last option, defying
the occupation. The PA was caught between a rock and a hard place.
Israel intensified its use of force to impose Barak's and Sharon's
humiliating dictates and Palestinian militants responded with
popular uprisings and resistance, combined later with suicide
bombings, leaving both Israelis and Palestinians in total insecurity.

The political and security polarization in Israel/Palestine has
anything but improved the chances for negotiations. Contrary to
Israeli accusations, the PA and its cronies had not instigated the
Intifada nor had they any interest in prolonging it. Quite the
opposite. Take, for example, their investment in tourism, which had
reached $3 billion, that has been almost totally lost because of
Israel's response to the Intifada.

Even in the Palestinian Israeli community political pressure has
been stepped up. For example, my own brother Azmi, a Palestinian
leader and a legislator in the Knesset, became an early victim of
post-Oslo Israeli injustice. After he declared Palestinian resistance
against occupation to be legitimate, as does the UN charter, his
parliamentary immunity was lifted by Israel's Attorney-General
Elyakim Rubinstein, apparently after consultations with the prime
minister and his intelligence services, and he was put on trial.

Instead of halting its settlement activity and implementing its
signed agreements, Israel intensified its occupation and oppression,
leaving the Palestinians ever more desperate. If life under
occupation has become impossible, then, an increasing number of
Palestinians responded, the price of maintaining the occupation
must also be made unbearable. Hence, when throwing stones was

met with live ammunition, there seemed no reason to hold back on suicide bombings. Instilling fear and uncertainty among Israelis, the suicide bombings also provided Israeli radicals with an opportunity to destroy the Palestinian political and governmental system and economy.

RESISTANCE AND SUICIDE BOMBINGS

In the face of this warmongering and in light of the failure of the peace process, the Palestinians have been left with only one option: to resist their occupiers while leaving the door open for a political process and international intervention that can bring reconciliation between the two peoples. Before the Palestinian factions even began their unfortunate suicide bombings and attacks inside Israel, their actions within their own Occupied Territories against the occupier had been considered terrorism by Barak, whose outrageous and excessive response set a precedent for Sharon's state terrorism. This response by Sharon seemed to gain legitimacy, especially in America and Israel, after September 11, in the context of the war on terrorism.

The Palestinian response to Israeli aggression and occupation has been legitimate resistance against foreign occupation. That does not include suicide bombings, nor do such actions constitute an effective strategy. Suicide bombings are, in fact, the direct result of the continuing occupation and the international community's abandonment of the Palestinians. Israel has a vast military superiority relative to poorly armed Palestinian militants, who fought the Israeli army without the support of the Palestinian security forces. This translated into a low intensity conflict, or what has come to be known as 'asymmetrical conflict'. Paradoxically, at the same time that the Israelis were bombarding Palestinian towns and assassinating political leaders, they were also demanding that the Palestinians hand over those presumed responsible for the assassination of an Israeli minister and the officials accused of smuggling arms on board the ship Karine-A. Arafat finally succumbed to pressure and, under Western security supervision, imprisoned them without a fair trial. The Israeli aggression continued as more Palestinians asked why there had not been more Karine-As smuggling arms to Palestinians for their self-defence. In short a culture of impunity has nurtured a culture of suicide bombings in Palestine.

Whilst the Israeli army continued its assault on Palestinian cities and camps in the Spring of 2002, the Palestinian leadership was asked to commit itself to protecting Israeli civilians, settlers, and soldiers in order that the Israeli army's siege of Arafat's headquarters and the autonomous Palestinian areas be lifted. The victims of occupation and aggression were asked to protect their occupiers and oppressors, a logic that defies common sense and human decency. Nonetheless, Arafat's acceptance of America's humiliating conditions was brushed aside as another ploy until he produced '100 percent' effort and '100 percent' results in the 'fight against terrorism'. Sharon had no interest in any accommodation with the Palestinians until they were on their knees begging for mercy. He went on to humiliate and incarcerate the Palestinians and their leaders, holding Arafat and the Palestinian people hostage to his occupation. In Peres' words to Sharon, Israel was 'needlessly humiliating' them.

In order that this logic of confrontation and war continue, the war on terrorism became Israel's alibi for the violence to come. Israel was defining its colonial war in the territories as one between democracy and terrorism, associating it with America's 'war on terrorism'. By oppression and occupation Israel had actually forged the enemy it claimed to be fighting, the suicide bombers. Ariel Sharon had promised the Israelis security, and the result a year later was unprecedented Israeli insecurity. His military policies failed on all levels - deterrence, prevention, and force. When Israeli assassinations of Palestinian leaders, F-16 bombardments, and invasions of Palestinian cities totally failed to deter the Palestinians,

Sharon's narrow logic of force was transformed into pure violence which engendered further violence.

* * * * * *

This book is primarily about the Oslo process experience, a process that obliged the Palestinians to make peace with their Israeli occupiers while that occupation still persisted. The Palestine Liberation Organization (PLO) leadership accepted this at Oslo and has signed seven interim agreements since then underlining their intention to live peacefully side-by-side with the Israeli state. The Palestinian Authority (PA) invested in major efforts to subdue the Islamist Hamas movement following the wave of suicide attacks in 1995 and 1996; these had been triggered by the Hebron massacre of 29 Palestinian worshipers carried out by Israeli religious fundamentalists. According to Israeli reports, almost the entire military arm of Hamas was eliminated. Extremist Muslim activists were imprisoned, and the PA seriously weakened the organizational infrastructure of the Islamist movements. However, instead of giving back the Occupied Territories to the Palestinians, Israel stepped up its illegal control of the West Bank by encircling the Palestinian population with a settlement network reinforced with bypass roads that only Israelis could use on newly confiscated land - roads that cut through the territories from all directions. After seven years, Israel had surrendered only 18 percent of the West Bank.

Ironically, the same week that Apartheid was being dismantled in South Africa at the beginning of May 1994, Israel began to erect a new system of Apartheid in Palestine with the signing of the Gaza-Jericho First Agreement. Unlike in South Africa, where the evil old ways of separation and the white acquisition of land had to stop immediately the negotiations began, in Palestine they intensified. In stark comparison with F.W. de Klerk's white government, which ceased land acquisition during the three-year negotiations with Nelson Mandela's African National Congress (ANC), the Israeli government of Yitzhak Rabin allowed the system of settlements on the West Bank and elsewhere to continue, as if the Oslo Agreement had never been signed.

The Apartheid government in South Africa had driven people off their farms, forced them to live in homelands, and then gave the land to whites. Successive Israeli governments, Labor or Likud, have applied these same policies of ethnic cleansing in historical Palestine, and the Israeli parliament has enshrined Israel's system of land exclusion, transfer, racism, and Apartheid in law. During the seven long years of the peace process, two laws prevailed in Palestine: one for the Jews and another for the Palestinians. Israelis had the freedom to move about, build, and expand, while the Palestinians were cooped up in encircled bantustans. Israelis had access to the land and expropriated more of it, while Palestinian access only diminished. Needless to say, Israel maintained a firm separation between Jewish settlers in the territories, who live under Israeli law and protection, and Palestinians, who live under shameful Palestinian legal and security structures. As in South Africa, where homeland chiefs were granted meaningless titles of sovereignty, so Israel was willing to give the Palestine National Authority (PNA) the appurtenances of sovereignty it could in no way exercise. Just as South Africa dominated and controlled the black homelands, so Israel has retained ultimate authority and control in and sovereignty over the autonomous enclaves. It also controls land, water, natural resources, and the movement of persons in the West Bank and Gaza, as well as the flow of goods into and out of the Palestinian bantustans. Again, as in South Africa, movement of workers was allowed only when the Israeli business community insisted upon it.

Meanwhile, persistent disparities between Jewish Israelis and Palestinians in terms of living standards, access to education, health, and employment continued during the Oslo process, and, in most cases, increased. Palestinian employment in Israel dwindled as unemployment among Palestinians reached 40 percent in Gaza - exactly as under South Africa's Apartheid - and the standard of living plummeted by 25 percent.

Of course, it was not merely material interest that spurred on Israeli policies. Like the Afrikaners, Israelis have proved to be in many ways irredeemably imprisoned in a siege mentality. Seven years on from the start of the Oslo process, the Palestinians, like all colonized nations, demanded that peace be conditional on ending the occupation and undoing the Apartheid system. They also rejected a final framework agreement modeled on the vague and general Oslo agreement. Hence, the outbreak of the second Intifada.

When the Intifada exploded in September 2000, the Israeli army was ready with elaborate plans to deal with it. For a number of years, Israel had been working on a military means to control the population and to curb the internal violence that might stem from the Oslo process. The Barak government engaged the Palestinians on two different fronts: on the ground it used collective punishment, excessive force, and political assassination in the West Bank and Gaza, while on the international front, it waged a disinformation campaign against the Palestinians in order to win the indispensable media war in the West, allowing it to recover its most precious title, that of 'Victim'. This was a difficult task in light of the recurring image of a mighty Israeli Goliath armed to the teeth fighting a stone-throwing Palestinian David. But Israel was not interested in winning the ground battles if it meant losing the war over international public opinion. Hence the campaign to discredit the Palestinian leadership and dehumanize the indigenous population of Palestine. The Israeli army killed some 100 Palestinian children in six months, but its chief of staff still went out of his way to accuse the Palestinians of being a terrorist entity.

The same policy was carried out on the other side of the Green Line dividing Israel from the Occupied Territories. Not until thirteen Palestinian Arab citizens of Israel had died and hundreds been injured at the hands of Israeli security forces in the first week of October 2000, did the world pay attention to the fact that there were also one million Palestinians inside Israel who lived as second-class citizens under a quasi-Apartheid system. An informal, state-sponsored neo-Apartheid has separated Israeli Jews from

Palestinians since the establishment of the Jewish state in 1948. Over the years, frequently referred to as a cancer and treated as a Fifth Column, these forgotten Palestinians have suffered enormously at the hands of Israel.

The Jewish state has continuously undermined the relationship of its Palestinian minority to the land, a basic characteristic of Apartheid. When Israeli Palestinians demonstrated their solidarity with their brethren across the border, the government immediately changed its buffer zone from the West Bank to the predominantly Palestinian areas of the Galilee and Triangle in the heart of Israel. The security orders of keeping the peace at any price were applied inside Israel in the same manner as they were executed in the Occupied Territories. The first and second chapters of this book cover the outbreak of the second Intifada and Israel's excessive use of violence against the Palestinians under occupation and those in Israel. But in order to understand the roots of the Intifada, one must look beyond the provocative visit of the infamous general, Ariel Sharon, to the Al-Aqsa Mosque.

The impasse in the diplomatic track was particularly damaging to the prospects for peace. For seven years the Oslo process continued to fail spectacularly as one ambiguous agreement after another was changed in order to keep the process alive and deepen Israeli domination in the occupied/autonomous territories. But such perseverance in the diplomatic process was possible only through the inflexible, aggressive, and coercive diplomacy of the one and only superpower, the United States of America.

The Clinton administration, which oversaw the entire 7-year process, holds primary responsibility for its utter failure. Washington manipulated and coerced the Palestinians to follow Israeli dictates throughout the process by taking the side of its ally, Israel, against its junior peace process partner, the Palestinians. The third and fourth chapters of this book discuss the impasse in the diplomatic process and America's role in its failure.

When the interim process was no longer useful for Israel, failing to nourish confidence and stability, the Israeli government moved to secure final status negotiations before it would surrender any more land or power to the PA. Two issues dominated the final talks' agenda: Jerusalem was visibly the thorniest issue in the negotiations and the question of the refugees was, covertly, the most complicated and the most difficult to resolve. The Palestinian refugees comprise the majority of the Palestinian people, numbering more than 3.7 million displaced persons, but at Israel's behest their plight remained taboo during the negotiations. It is not surprising that such mockery of the peace process could go on with little commentary in the West if, according to Palestinian scholar Edward Said, 92 percent of the Western electorate still do not know that there is a Law of Return for Jews only, and that Israel was built on the ruins of Palestinian society.

When the curtains finally closed on the theatrics of the peace process at Camp David, Barak claimed that Israel had done all it could to reach out for peace, but that the Palestinians had rejected Israel's 'generous' offer. Nothing could be further from the truth. As Robert Malley wrote in the *New York Review of Books*, the offer was neither Israeli, nor was it generous. In fact, it was not an offer. Clinton did all the bargaining because Barak refused to commit himself or to give the American president sufficient space for maneuver. When the final status negotiations finally put the ordeal of the refugees on the agenda of Camp David, Israel refused to admit any moral, legal, or political responsibility for their displacement and refrained from committing itself to any compensation or repatriation. Instead, on January 1, 2001, the Knesset introduced two new landmark decisions supported by all of its Jewish members. The first vehemently opposed the Palestinians' Right of Return, and the second approved the privatisation of state lands, which legally belong to those 3.7 million Palestinian refugees who continue to languish in the Occupied Territories and neighboring states, and whose Right of Return the Knesset and government have repeatedly rejected, although it is an inalienable right.

Here they were, all the upbeat Zionist members of parliament, looking energized by the biggest loot of the century and, as in times gone by, the greedy conquerors divided up the spoils of their conquest among themselves, leaving their victims to the misery of the refugee camps. But that's not all. Jerusalem was the thorniest issue at the Camp David summit. And although Israel broke the taboo on Jerusalem by agreeing to hand over to the Palestinians effective sovereignty in certain neighborhoods in the city, it nonetheless insisted on annexing all the illegal settlements in the city built after its occupation in 1967. It also demanded that the Palestinians accept a barter agreement, one that swaps Israeli compromises in East Jerusalem for Palestinian renunciation of the Right of Return.

Chapters five and six address those two central issues whose resolution is indispensable to a historic reconciliation between Israelis and Palestinians.

Meanwhile, and in order to contain Palestinian discontent and obtain the conformity of their leadership, Washington ensured the flow of international aid to the Palestinian National Authority (PNA), which amounted to around 3 billion dollars over the seven years. However, as the World Bank has testified, the economic situation has anything but improved for the Palestinians. In fact, it has deteriorated badly because of Israel's imposed closures on the newly formed cantons in the Occupied Territories. The world, so intoxicated by the diplomatic celebrations and successes of Oslo, has paid little if any attention to the ongoing suffering under the new Apartheid system. On the other hand, Israel profited enormously from its impunity and from the new international economic relations after the accords were signed and the Arab boycott was lifted. This was well planned through the transforming of Israel's colonial relations in the territories prior to Oslo into relations of Palestinian dependency vis-à-vis Israel.

The most obvious example of this disfiguration of the peace process has been Israel's obsession with security and its continued colonization and settlement in the West Bank and Gaza. The territorial integrity of those territories was to be kept intact until Israel eventually evacuated its forces. However, as chapters seven and eight show, the policy of physical or demographic separation from the Palestinians, coupled with further Israeli settlement and economic expansion on the ground, has transformed a 26-year occupation into a system of Apartheid. Ultimately the continuous occupation and oppression led to the radicalization and theologization of Israeli society that fell under the spell or the influence of the radical settlers. For secular Israeli liberals, the settler movement with its religious fervor has been anathema to democracy. Settler leaders have called for putting Leftists in jail as threats were made against what the new Right have termed 'the Oslo criminals', with fascist wall slogans warning: 'No Leftists, No Casualties,' 'No Arabs, No Casualties,' even though the Peace Now leadership and the liberal Meretz leaders went out of their way to declare that refusing to serve in the territories with the Israeli army was 'undemocratic'. By April 2002, over 400 Israelis had registered their refusal to serve in the territories and 35 were given jail sentences. This was the best development since the beginning of the Intifada.

Meanwhile, the settlement drive and settler ideology emerges as a cornerstone of the modern Israeli national identity. The settlement-driven politics and their current violent manifestations have jumped over ethnic and religious divides in the country to mould a new 'Israelism' based strictly on new Jewish nationalism. The settlers and their allies are reproducing Israel according to their own image: a theocracy in permanent conflict. Under Sharon's rule, and with the explicit support of the Bush administration, this process is increasingly becoming an irreversible and destructive self-fulfilling prophecy.

VIOLENCE

I

THE SECOND INTIFADA

When the negotiations began, the Israeli army was in control of a
narrow strip in Lebanon just west of northern Galilee which
enclosed fourteen villages ... [The prime minister] wrote in his diary,
'In my opinion we should sign regardless of the Syrian withdrawal.'
He reckoned such a move would strengthen Israel's political position
in general ... embarrass Syria ... it will increase the pressure on the
Syrians and facilitate a move onto the West Bank – if it should be
necessary. The military disagreed at first, but the prime minister,
who was also minister of defense, decided to go ahead.
TOM SEGEV, *THE FIRST ISRAELIS* (1949)

This was not in the time of Ehud Barak, but of David Ben-
Gurion. Five decades of independence, five wars, and a decade
of the peace process later, Israel – a nuclear power, the most
powerful country in the region, and one of the twenty richest
countries in the world – remains hostage to those same illusions and
ambitions that characterized its early years. When he withdrew from
South Lebanon in May 2000, Barak followed the same logic that
Ben-Gurion had done fifty years before, namely to concentrate
Israel's energy to its east in order to insure its interests in the West
Bank and in East Jerusalem.

However, knowing that the world has changed since the late
forties, Barak understood that Israel was no longer capable of
repeating the 1948 or 1967 mass ethnic cleansing of Palestine, and

that it could not occupy more land. Israel has also learned that mass expulsions, occupation, and annexation solved no problems. In fact, they complicated Israel's presence in the region and as a member of the world community. Instead, Israel has tried to encircle and dominate the remaining three and half million Palestinians in historical Palestine through settlements and military means during thirty-three years of occupation, but has failed to attain further control over the land and its people.

Seven years of the Oslo process also failed to legitimize Israel's domination of the West Bank and Gaza. The Palestinian upheaval, triggered by the visit of Israeli Rightist leader Ariel Sharon to the Al-Aqsa Mosque on September 28, 2000, speaks volumes about the failure of the last seven transitional agreements to ameliorate living conditions in Palestine.

For seven long years, the Palestinian National Authority (PNA) did the dirty work for Israel. It collaborated with the Labor and Likud governments to fight Palestinian 'terrorism,' and any form of resistance to occupation, in order to maintain calm during the initial five-year transitional period mandated by the Oslo agreement. The PNA launched a campaign of oppression against Islamist figures and activists, permitted the torture of opposition leaders and journalists, and allowed the humiliation and arrest of political opponents of the Oslo process, including Legislative Council members. The PNA also became hostile toward non-governmental organizations (NGOs), which were demanding accountability and respect for human rights. The Palestinian leadership had to accept Israel's humiliating security conditions in order to earn its diplomatic 'generosity,' but Israel's political stinginess and continuous blackmail put the PNA in a bind. As popular resistance to its rule mounted, the PNA was forced to choose between doing the 'master's bidding' or attending to the needs and wishes of its own people. For a long time, it defended its actions as the means to a justified end, but as the first five years passed, the promised happy ending never came. Two extra years brought more of the same.

Inevitably, the light at the end of the tunnel dimmed after Camp David II's failure, forcing the PNA to step aside and to allow the people to express themselves freely.

Oslo had come to be the problem, not the solution. The official goal of a 'just, lasting, and comprehensive peace settlement' was transformed into unjust, temporary, and partial agreements leading to complete Palestinian dissatisfaction and frustration. There was no more room for transitional or temporary arrangements. It was time to evacuate the majority of the Occupied Territories as stipulated in the Oslo agreement, and as expected of Israel since it had originally occupied the lands in 1967.

The diplomatic impasse and the excessive use of force following Sharon's provocative visit to Al-Aqsa Mosque paved the way for the new rupture in the Occupied Territories. But it is Barak, not Sharon, who is to blame for the outbreak of the second Intifada. Barak commanded the army and headed the government, not Sharon. It came as no surprise that the Israeli prime minister repeatedly asked Sharon to be his partner in a 'national unity' or, later, in an 'emergency government.' In other words, a war government. Were it not for opposition from Likud activists loyal to his rival Binyamin Netanyahu, Barak would have succeeded. Eighteen months after taking office, despite having started his tenure with the support of some seventy-five parliamentarians, he ended up with a minority government commanding no more than thirty seats in the Knesset.

Once Barak failed in his promises as prime minister, he immediately turned to the means most familiar to him, the military.

Israel's war against the Palestinians was influenced by two considerations: internal pressure which brought about the launch of the military campaign, and the media's reporting which played a large role in the international reaction. Hence, Israel fought the Palestinians on two fronts, with the military and in the media. Within Israel, rightist populism, threats from settlers, and blackmail by the centrist parties have all pressured the government to 'let the IDF [Israel Defense Force] win,' Milosevic-style if necessary. Barak was told by settlement leaders either to use more force or risk escalation, including the intervention of settlers, in the confrontation and his own eventual downfall. Barak needed no encouragement when it came to force. As a general, he always approached political problems with military solutions. Externally, however, Barak couldn't afford to appear like the Serb leader Milosevic in the eyes of his Western counterparts, ultimately destroying everything America had worked towards. He wasn't about to make the same mistakes that the Serbs had made in Bosnia and Kosovo, which led to their isolation, punishment, and defeat.

As a result, Barak pursued a two-faced policy. Using the air force and tanks to bombard Palestinian towns, he led an 'asymmetric war' against the Palestinians in an effort to appease the radicals. But externally, the policy was defined as one of 'restraint' in order to avoid international condemnation or action. The government used a special emergency media campaign, a sort of rapid-deployment media force, to discredit Palestinian claims and to vindicate Israeli violence. Pursuing a fine line, Barak slammed the door hard on the Palestinians' hands, while making sure that they were still able to sign an agreement with Israel. This was not a policy of 'breaking bones,' as was pursued by Yitzhak Rabin during the first Intifada, but one of breaking the national will of the Palestinian people. In a rather sarcastic tone, the correspondent of the daily *Haaretz* in the Occupied Territories wrote:

> Israel's policy of restraint has led to the following results over the past six weeks: up until yesterday morning, 179 Palestinians have been killed by the IDF, 48 of whom were aged 17 or under; about 8,000 have been injured, including some 1,200 who will be crippled for life.[1]

The following six weeks witnessed more of the same. However, the Palestinians suffered not only from the violence of the Israeli military, but also from the colonialist settlers. The authoritative Palestinian Society for the Protection of Human Rights and the Environment (LAW) reported numerous settler attacks against Palestinians, at times in the army's presence or under their protection. These attacks included maiming, torture, shooting, blocking of roads, and killings. In fact, prior to the Intifada's commencement, LAW released numerous reports of Palestinians being lynched by settlers.

The story of Issam Hamad is representative of the actions of the settlers. On October 8, settlers from Halamish kidnapped 36-year-old Mr. Hamad while he was traveling to his village of Um Safa. When his body was retrieved, Issam's face was burned, his hands were broken, his back was bruised, and the autopsy revealed the cause of death as a blow to the head with a sharp object. During his funeral the next day in Ramallah, the marching Palestinians learned of the 'presence' of two Israeli soldiers at a Palestinian police station. The station was attacked and the two soldiers were brutally killed. They were believed to be members of a special Israeli unit – Mustaribeen – responsible for the capture and assassination of many Palestinians.[2]

ON THE GROUND: ISRAEL'S LAND WAR

From the beginning of the Oslo process, Israel developed and tested a number of contingency plans, including 'Field of Thorns,' which envisaged a scenario of reoccupying the West Bank and Gaza, according to a report in *Jane's Intelligence Review*. During the negotiations at Camp David, the army began training according to a new plan, 'Magic Tune,' which foresaw a scenario of mass rioting that would require a full-scale military mission to manage a low-intensity conflict. Moreover, a full-scale war involving the setting up of a new military administration in the Occupied Territories was also studied by the Israeli army under the code, 'Distant World.'[3]

Barak prepared for the outbreak of hostilities when he anticipated mass Palestinian disturbances following a unilateral declaration of independence that never occurred. With the first sign of confrontation, 'Operation Ebb and Flow' was pulled out of the drawer by the Israeli government and harshly implemented by the Israeli military. In order to insure maximum control and avoid Israeli casualties, especially among the military, Barak took the following steps:

1. Deployment of a special unit of snipers able to target field leaders (agitators, including children). They were responsible for most of the deaths in the first three weeks.
2. Allowing the military to use M-24s and other new weapons instead of the M-16, insuring maximum casualties.
3. Use of formidable force, including tanks and aircraft, similar to that used in Lebanon over the course of eighteen years of occupation. This included assassination and kidnapping to intimidate and frighten both civilians and political leaders.
4. The selective imposition of closures and, at times, the complete closure of the West Bank, but without leading to large-scale starvation and without cutting off electricity or water, which could incite the entire population and bring about international intervention.
5. Assassination of political leaders charged with organizing the Intifada, especially those political leaders who organized the activists of the mainstream Fateh party in the West Bank and Gaza. This was done either through the special forces or through the air force's surgical strikes.
6. Clearing the way for the takeover of certain strategic locations and, perhaps, preparing for the annexation to Israel of large areas of the West Bank.

All of these Israeli measures amounted to state-sponsored terrorism. Israel's operations were similar to those it had conducted over the last eighteen years of occupation in southern Lebanon. Unlike his predecessor, Netanyahu, General Barak's military concerns took the lion's share of his defunct statesmanship. However, Barak had another way to measure his success as a leader. In the IDF's 'quantitative index,' which measures the degree to which the IDF can reduce the number of Israeli casualties, the results of 'Operation High and Low Tides' were deemed 'pretty good:' in the first week, one dead, compared to sixteen during the 'Western Wall Tunnel' clashes in September 1996.[4]

Aside from the high casualties, hundreds dead and thousands injured, there was another price to be paid by all Palestinians as a result of Israel's oppression. The closures blew a huge hole in the Palestinian economy, an economy already deteriorating since Oslo began seven years previously. In the first month, the Israeli siege cost the Palestinians at least US$346 million according to Palestinian estimates ($250 million according to the UN), and the same again in the following months. Unemployment tripled overnight and farmers were losing $2 million each day. Most new business ventures suffered tremendously as the business environment deteriorated due to uncertainty, instability, and violence.[5]

There was no doubt that the Palestinians were no match for Israel and, as a result, would suffer dearly on the ground. But the longer the Intifada lasted, the more Israel seemed to lose overall, as instability became a factor in its own political and economic life. The Israeli tourist industry was severely affected as long-term reservations were cancelled. The stock market suffered, and Israeli companies trading on the New York Stock Exchange were badly hit. Nonetheless, Barak and the head of the Bank of Israel claimed that growth would be only marginally affected. In comparison to Palestine, Israel had nothing to worry about in terms of its economy.

As a result of severe violations of Palestinians' human and civil rights, the United Nations Human Rights Commission (UNHRC) adopted a resolution on October 19, 2000, condemning Israel's 'disproportionate and indiscriminate use of force' against Palestinian civilians. After hearing the report by UNHRC Special Rapporteur Giorgio Giacomelli, which accused Israel of having 'drastically escalated the use of force against the civilian population,' the Commission accused Israel of war crimes and crimes against humanity.[6]

Over a month later, the UN Commissioner for Human Rights, Mary Robinson, reported on the continued use of 'excessive force' by Israel in the Occupied Territories and condemned Israel's occupation and illegal settlements, blaming Israel for the suffering of the Palestinians. In practical terms, Ms Robinson called for the legal accountability of all who were engaged in the use of lethal force, and for international monitors to be placed in the occupied Palestinian territories.[7]

Attempts by the international community to bring pressure to bear on Israel failed as a result of a US veto. After an ill-prepared attempt in Paris to stop the violence, an even more fruitless summit in Sharm el-Sheikh brought together Presidents Clinton and Mubarak, Chairman Arafat, Prime Minister Barak, UN Secretary General Kofi Annan, and European Higher Commissioner on Foreign Policy Javier Solana. This summit too failed to stop the violence.

The Sharm el-Sheikh Memorandum called for President Clinton to set up a commission to investigate the causes of the Intifada. Senior Israeli diplomats claimed that 'there is no reason for concern' because the make-up of the commission was 'comfortable' for Israel, and they added that its mandate did not leave much leeway for it to become a political weapon the Palestinians could use. Israel once again enjoyed impunity in the international arena.[8]

THE INTERNATIONAL FRONT: ISRAEL'S MEDIA WAR

On the international front, Israel had to undo the damage caused by the media. In today's world, the camera can affect the outcome of an asymmetric war no less than the gun. The Barak government had to offset the effect of the cameras, a natural ally of the weak Palestinians – the Davids carrying slingshots. Understanding this all too well, the Israelis set up an emergency media campaign fulfilling the role of a Rapid Deployment Media Force, meant to undo the inherited 'disadvantage' of its prowess and the way it is reflected on international radio and television. The Palestinians, on the other hand, and as usual, played out their Intifada to the full instead of taking advantage of the new tools of the global era. At times they did more harm than good to their just cause of resisting the occupation, as in the case of the bloody lynching of the two Israeli soldiers in the West Bank town of Ramallah.

From the outset it was evident, in the words of Ron Ben Yishai, the military correspondent of Israel's most circulated newspaper, *Yedioth Ahranot*, that Israel's military could not convince a Western journalist that when a tank confronts a child, the tank operates 'within its right' and the child is the 'aggressor,' and, therefore, it should adopt an alternative strategy. Hence the fabricated stories of the cruel, unloving, and cowardly Palestinian parents who send their children to die for their cause and the bloody 'Tanzim', an invented paramilitary organization driven by hatred of Israel.

In order to confuse the Western media and blur the distinction between Israel's war on civilians and children, and a conventional war against a standing army, the Barak government went on the offensive, blaming the occupied – the victims of its terror and aggression – on two fronts: the family, or the parents, who 'encourage their children' to fight the adults' fights; and the Tanzim, the presumably radical military organ of Fateh, the principal political party, that threatens the stability of the region and American interests. These are the new enemies which must be dealt with firmly. Cynically, Barak pretended that no equivalence could be drawn between the moral concerns of Israel, a 'democracy,' and those of the Palestinians, who opposed peace.

Paradoxically, these were the same allegations made by the British Mandate forces against the Jews in the 1940s. French journalist and author Charles Enderlin wrote in his book on the secret negotiations between Palestinians and Israelis[9] that in 1945 the British Mandate forces shot at Jewish demonstrators in Tel Aviv, killing six and wounding dozens, eighteen of them children between the ages of eight and sixteen, and fourteen between the ages of sixteen and twenty. On the second day, the British press reported that Jewish parents sent their children to die for them. Two Jewish doctors were pictured in the Zionist paper, *Davar*, treating a child shot by British bullets: one doctor is telling the other what great marksmen those soldiers were, hitting such a small creature from such a distance. The newspaper was closed down. Today, fifty-five years later, a repetition of the same kind of colonialist and racist remarks and reactions that the British used against the Jews is deployed by Israelis and their friends against the Palestinians. They are not worth comment.[10]

Nonetheless, Israel has succeeded in this campaign. Palestinians were suddenly having to defend their love for their children. From a French comedian to the Queen of Sweden, to the local elementary schools in Western countries, Israeli propaganda succeeded in blaming Palestinian mothers for their families' suffering instead of blaming the occupation forces that fired on their children indiscriminately. Needless to say, more adults than children died during the Intifada while resisting the occupation. One only needs to visit the cramped refugee camps of Gaza and the West Bank to see these children's living conditions and how little, if anything, a parent can do to control the young ones who confront the Israeli aggressors. In short, while the Israeli military was killing and wounding children, the Israeli government was blaming their mourning parents for their deaths – and it almost succeeded. This was one of the most ironic turns of events in the Intifada.

As for the 'Tanzim,' the story is even more bizarre. The whole theory of Tanzim emerged in October 2000 after Israel began to lose the media war, in spite of deploying its heavy canons – such as Shimon Peres, Yossi Beilin, Amos Oz, and other 'doves' – in the media. Even US Secretary of State Madeleine Albright praised Israeli 'restraint' and demanded that 'the Palestinians stop throwing stones.' But none of this could efface the image of Israeli soldiers killing twelve-year-old Muhammad Dura in his father's lap. Barak suddenly showed up in a press conference and spat out names of Fateh activists, demanding that Arafat curb their violent activity against Israel. Since then, the Israeli and world press have talked of a 'military arm' of Fateh, calling it the 'Tanzim.'

In fact, 'Tanzim' is simply how Palestinians refer to Fateh – Arafat's party that won the elections in the West Bank and Gaza. In Palestine, people refer to Fateh, the biggest of all organizations, as 'the organization,' in Arabic, 'Al-Tanzim.' However, that is neither important nor relevant today, because the facts have become irrelevant. The facts are the first victim of Israeli propaganda and aggression. The young people who fired upon the Israelis, a hundred at most, are not necessarily from Fateh, nor do they claim to be, although many Fateh organizers have been armed. Whoever did fire on the Israelis, they certainly did not represent an organized force that warrented such over-reaction. A new security threat has been invented, dramatized, and called the Tanzim. Ironically, the besieged and humiliated Palestinians began to believe the story themselves, reckoning that they had a military answer to the occupation. A child would respond to a journalist's question by claiming to be a member of Tanzim, not realizing the security implications of such an admission.

Until the Intifada broke out, and Israel began to attack and assassinate local Fateh leaders, there was no coherent, organized, military group called Tanzim. As Marwan Barghuti confirmed to me in a private conversation, most of those responsible for the shootings have been recently released prisoners from Israeli jails, others are known car thieves and outlaws, while still others are committed fighters whose families suffered and continue to suffer at the hands of Israel and its occupation forces, particularly in Areas B and C.[11] But these young Palestinians do not constitute an organization, and no pyramid-like organization has been giving orders to shoot. By the second week of the Intifada, Fateh leaders began to fear for their lives and the lives of their families, especially after Israel started targeting them as if they were Hezbollah fighters. This was more difficult to justify than the assassination of Islamist Hamas leaders, whom Israel succeeded in labeling as terrorists.

Sadly, many of the targeted Fateh leaders have led the civil campaign of liberalism and secularism in society, and they have at times spearheaded an anti-corruption campaign within the PNA. In fact, they are the 'local' West Bank and Gaza progressive forces that stood against corrupt leaders who came to Palestine after 1993. They also stood against Hamas and other opponents of the peace process, advocating giving the Oslo process a chance. But today, after the process has already failed, they are being blamed for its failure. Ironically, were it not for Fateh, the peace process would not have held for so long, even though its leadership was not entirely convinced of the utility of the Oslo process after witnessing the suffering that resulted from the implementation of Oslo's security clauses and the lack of implementation of its political aspects.

Needless to say, by the second month, the local Fateh leadership emerged as the backbone of the 'peaceful' Intifada, and the engine behind its steadfastness. In its turn, the Intifada strengthened this important local component of the mainstream Palestinian party. It is as if Israel realized a self-fulfilling prophecy. The voices of the likes of Marwan Barghuti, a Fateh leader and legislative council member, were very effective in maintaining the resistance spirit of the Intifada. The role of organized groups within Fateh became increasingly important in the new Intifada, although there has not been the massive participation there was in the first Intifada of 1987–1993. In the absence of direct contact with Israeli soldiers or settlers in the densely populated cities and refugee camps of Area A, the role of small, organized resistance groups became central to the disruption of the occupation and its illegal settlements.

The Israeli incitement against the local Fateh leadership as a new danger to regional stability took disproportionate dimensions. A story appearing in a well-known defense magazine claimed that Tanzim was one of three suspects in the bombing of the American ship U.S.S. Cole on the shores of Yemen. This propaganda gave Barak renewed licence to oppress, kill, and declare war on Palestinian demonstrators with America's blessing. In fact, on November 15, 2000, the day Israeli forces killed eight people, President Clinton asked Congress for $450 million in American military aid to Israel.

The following day, a story in the daily *Haaretz* headlined 'Fifteen Fateh men held for role in shootings, Barak: "The IDF will strike at anyone who harms Israelis,"' showed how Israel fabricated its Fateh story. The story went on to report how the commander of the IDF oversaw the operation in which arrests were carried out in three villages – Kusra, Talfit, and El Mouaier. 'In all cases, the Fateh activists surrendered without a fight after their homes were surrounded by the IDF troops ... Prime Minister Ehud Barak commended the operation yesterday.' However the story ends with the following claim, 'Contrary to some reports yesterday, it appears that those arrested were not involved in the drive-by shooting attacks that left two soldiers and one settler dead on Monday.' On the same day, another story reported that 'The air force attacked houses in Beit Jala, Tulkarm, Jericho, Nablus, and Hebron ... The attacks followed a stormy day of demonstrations across the territories in which eight Palestinians were killed and dozens wounded.'

In sum, Israel's military continued to use disproportionate and arbitrary force against Palestinian civilian and political activists with the complicity of the media, almost totally recruited to do the propaganda work for the government. In most cases, only Amira Haas, the *Haaretz* correspondent in the Occupied Territories, would report a different kind of story. One such case was demonstrated in an intelligence report on December 7, 2000 where she wrote: 'Four Palestinians were killed eleven days ago in an offensive action by the Israel Defense Forces in the Gaza Strip. Initial army reports spoke of a Fateh cell, but testimony by a taxi driver from Rafah and other witnesses tell a different story.' This has been a frequent recurrence throughout the Intifada.[12]

Although three months into the Intifada Israel had won all the battles against the Palestinians, it began to lose the war it launched against them. This was, to a certain extent, expected. Israeli army and intelligence services knew that Israel could not win a war against a Palestinian uprising, at least not in any internationally recognized fashion. Before the second Intifada broke out, former Shin Bet head Ami Ayalon commented to *Nekuda*, the official publication of the Yesha Council of West Bank and Gaza Strip settlers, 'We lost the first Intifada and we will also lose the next one.' He later warned that Israel could not afford to be an 'Apartheid' state.[13]

THE INTIFADA: A BREAK WITH OSLO

Israeli and American efforts to facilitate Israeli domination, or what was referred to as the 'rule of law,' were destroyed by the Intifada. All of Oslo's security arrangements failed to provide the necessary security as the PNA refused to quell demonstrations against the occupation. Israel expected the PNA to act as a client, or worse, as a buffer security zone such as provided by the Southern Lebanese Army (SLA), which had been armed and financed by Israel to function as a buffer between its occupation and the resistance in South Lebanon. Obviously, even if such a maneuver worked for a while, substituting a Palestinian policeman for an Israeli soldier was not going to bring peace or stability to the Occupied Territories. In the process, the Palestinians have paid a heavy price in human suffering that will take decades to heal. The second Intifada, like the first one, has witnessed thousands of permanently injured individuals. Few families have escaped some sort of humiliation, imprisonment, injury, or death.

The second Intifada has put an end to the illusion of Oslo's success. In attacking the most damaging barrier to peace, namely the settlements, it put on hold the building of new settlements, put their whole existence in doubt, and disrupted the entire network of by-pass roads (special roads built for the Israelis linking the settlements). The Intifada proved that regardless of all the Israeli security precautions, the settlements were not safe, nor was safe passage to them secure. It also underlined the fact that any initiatives for peace should discount the settlements dispersed all over the West Bank, and limit any proposed solution for them to no less than 5 percent of the territories close to the Green Line. This 5 percent could eventually be exchanged for territories within Israel proper, as was proposed by President Clinton in mid-December, 2000.

Although the Palestinians improvised the second Intifada, their spontaneous actions were obviously not aimless. This time, unlike with previous uprisings and demonstrations, the aim was very definitely to go beyond the Oslo accords and to demand independence, or rather an end to the occupation. It is also realistic. As in most other processes of decolonization, violence unfortunately seems to be a necessary element. This is no different. The picture of Muhammad Dura killed in his father's lap in Gaza, like the other horrific pictures of a naked Vietnamese girl hit by napalm, the grave of raped nuns in El Salvador, and a journalist murdered in Nicaragua, ushered in a new era of absurd levels of violence.

Palestinian dissatisfaction aside, the central problem in the region before and after the Intifada has not been Palestinian *per se*; it is an Israeli problem. Israel is not ready for a decolonization that will end its military control of the Occupied Territories. Israel opted to take Gaza out of Tel Aviv,[14] but not Tel Aviv out of Gaza. More importantly, Israel is incapable, it would seem, of taking Gaza out of its political culture. For Israel, Palestine has proven once more to be an existential problem that leads it to see the conflict with the Palestinians as a zero-sum-game, where Palestinian gains are Israel's losses and vice versa. Under such conditions, coexistence really means domination and no diplomatic process can bring about peace and stability. In this context, the Intifada has not been a security problem to be dealt with through force; it has a clear political message that needs to be listened to, and the plight of the people should be heard. The Intifada broke out because of the impasse in the negotiations, but its roots are ingrained in the occupation and the Oslo process that was meant to put an end to the century-old conflict.

It took a leading Israeli sociologist, Baruch Kimmerling, to explain to Israelis that:

After some 35 years of occupation, exploitation, uprooting and degradation, the Palestinian people have the right to use force to oppose the Israeli occupation, which, in itself, is the brutal exercise of force. Millions of people cannot be forced today to remain under the subjugation of a foreign occupier. Anyone who thinks otherwise is merely indulging in a pipe dream. (*Haaretz*, June 6, 2001)

Ironically, it took the Palestinians forty years to prove that they are the David of the conflict and Israel the Goliath, and now it seems they need many more years to prove that David is not misbehaving, he is only reclaiming his freedom.

NOTES

1. Amira Hass, 'A different definition of "restraint,"' *Haaretz*, November 15, 2000.
2. *People's Rights*, October 2000, pp. 16–18, LAW, Ramallah.
3. Cited in Shraga Elam, 'Peace with violence or transfer,' *Between the Lines* (Jerusalem monthly), December 2000, pp. 11–13.
4. Amir Oren, *Haaretz*, October 3, 2000.
5. Eric Silver, *The Independent*, 6 November 2000.
6. This resolution was passed within two weeks of UN Security Council Resolution (UNSCR) 1322 (October 7) and an October 20 General Assembly Resolution, both of which condemned the 'excessive use of force' by Israel. The UNHRC resolution called for the establishment of a 'human rights inquiry commission' and asked UN High Commissioner for Human Rights Mary Robinson to investigate further the severe human rights violations committed by Israel.
7. *Miftah*, November 28, 2000. According to the special report prepared by the UN Special Rapporteur Giorgio Giacomelli, the lethal use of force by Israel resulted in some 85 deaths within the first two weeks, or the same number as were killed in four months of the Intifada in 1987–1988. Many of the deaths resulted from snipers shooting from long distances as well as from the paramilitary forces organized by the settlers. The report estimated that up to 3,700 Palestinians were injured by Israeli forces, 40 percent under 18 years of age. It also noted that 40 percent of the injures were in the head, 20 percent in the chest, 20 percent in the abdomen, and 20 percent in the extremities and back. Half resulted from live ammunition, with the remaining injuries caused by rubber-coated metal bullets and tear gas (about 10 percent). Moreover, the report elaborated on the use of excessive force including

'machine guns, deployed tanks, fired rockets, and anti-tank missiles' in addition to firing from 'helicopter gunships and naval vessels.'

8. Aluf Ben, *Haaretz*, December 7, 2000.

9. Paix ou guerres. Les secrets des négociations israélo-arabes 1917–1997, Stock, Paris, 1997, pp. 51–52.

10. Cited in *Le Monde Diplomatique*, November 2000, p. 13.

11. As stipulated in Oslo II, Areas A are those under Palestinian security and civilian control, Areas B are those where the Palestine National Authority has civilian authority and Israel exercises security control, while Areas C are under full Israeli military and civilian control.

12. Amira Haas, *Haaretz*, November 16, 2000.

13. Cited in Yoel Marcus, 'The "bedrock of our existence" returns,' *Haaretz*, October 3, 2000.

14. A Rabin/Barak reference to the number of Gazans working in Tel Aviv.

2

ISRAEL'S 'ENEMY WITHIN': THE MILLION FORGOTTEN PALESTINIANS

If we had been one army, not several armies, and if we had acted according to one strategic plan, we would have been able to 'empty' the [Palestinian] population of the upper Galilee, Jerusalem and the road to it, Ramllah, Ludda, southern Palestine in general and the Negev in particular.

DAVID BEN GURION (IDF ARCHIVES)

Asil Assli was eighteen years old. Born in the Galilee of Palestinian parents, he spoke Arabic and Hebrew. He had an Israeli identity card – but Israel defines itself as the state of the Jewish people, Israel is not the state of its citizens. Asil was brilliant, top of his class, won prizes in sciences, but he had no scientific future in Israel, which discriminates against its Arab citizens. He was the perfect student, according to his teachers at the Mar Elias missionary secondary school. But none of that mattered to the Israeli soldiers who spotted Asil from afar, as he demonstrated with the young men of the small village of Arraba in solidarity with their Palestinian brethren on the other side of the Green Line. Asil was murdered in the olive groves while his mother was watching from a distance. Paradoxically, the young Asil wore a t-shirt printed with an olive branch and the words 'Seeds of Peace,' referring to an American youth camp for Jewish–Arab dialogue that he attended every year. The security forces spotted Asil as he helped an injured friend shot by their bullets, and decided to teach him a lesson. They ran after him unconcerned by the cries of his mother, and as soon as they caught him, they hit him with their M-16s, and then shot him in cold blood at zero distance. As they emerged from between the olive trees, they told his parents 'now you can go get him.' Asil went out to voice his anger at the Israeli shooting of Muhammad Dura who was killed huddled against the body of his father in Gaza, only to be murdered in front of his own parents. Later in the week, Mar Elias remembered its 'martyr', who joined at least thirteen more dead and thousands injured. Asil's father told journalists he still 'believed in Jewish–Arab coexistence'!¹

OCTOBER 2000: THE ISRAELI PALESTINIANS' LONELY RISING

This is, more or less, the dilemma of the million-strong Palestinian minority in the state of Israel. A new chapter in their relationship with the state opened following the October oppression and as a result of the government's severe and racist reaction to their protest.² In fact, as Israel went to war against its Palestinian citizens, killing thirteen and injuring hundreds in a matter of a few days, it immediately released years of pent-up violence. The Palestinians could not be indifferent to the death of their brethren in the West Bank and Gaza.

The Higher Monitoring Committee, an informal umbrella group that represents Israel's Palestinian minority, called for a general strike two days after Sharon's visit to the Al-Aqsa Mosque, and in response to the earlier killing of six Palestinians at the mosque in Jerusalem. The televised pictures of the cold-blooded killing of twelve-year-old Muhammad Dura in Gaza sent shivers through the Arab communities who poured into the streets to express their anger. Israel's harsh response was anything but improvised. Under orders from Barak, the security services had already prepared a contingency plan to confront the Palestinian citizens of Israel in case they dared to show solidarity with the proposed unilateral declaration of a Palestinian state on the other side of the Green Line. Once the peaceful protest started, the plan was executed by the infamous police chief, Alik Ron, resulting in three dead on October 1 and tens injured. To justify the disproportionate use of lethal force, the demonstrations were referred to as an 'uprising,' or even 'revolt,' by Israeli ministers and commentators.

Paradoxically, the harshness with which the security forces responded to Arab protests within Israel blurred the Green Line separating Israel from the Palestinian territories. It also reversed Barak's original intention of 'separating' physically from 'the Palestinians': them over there, us over here. The Palestinians of Israel figured squarely in the heart of the emerging reality as they rose in defense of their 'national and religious' symbols. Instead of calming the situation peacefully and containing the protest within democratically accepted norms, the government used the same severe measures it had used against those under occupation, hence blurring the difference between the Palestinians under occupation and those within Israel proper. In fact, one Arab lawyer from the Arab NGO Adalah, a law group representing Palestinian detainees, told me privately that the police considered the Arab areas in the Triangle and Galilee were to be dealt with as in Areas A in the West Bank.

All over the country, and wherever they resided, even in the mixed Jewish and Arab cities, the Palestinians' protest was further inflamed by Israel's bloody response. This led to more killings, some quite systematic, and to ethnic attacks by the Jewish majority against the Arab minority, with little interference from the state in defense of the Arabs. In Tiberias Jews attacked and destroyed a 200-year-old mosque, while lynchings of Arabs went on unabated in the first two weeks of October 2000. Shops, houses, and individuals were attacked and Jewish mobs even targeted Jewish businesses that employed Arabs. In Arab Nazareth, attacks by a mob of hundreds of Jews from neighboring Natsrat Elit lead to three deaths and tens injured as the Israeli forces joined the mob in their assaults on inhabitants. A day earlier, another Jewish mob carrying torches and bats approached the house of Arab leader and Member of Parliament Azmi Bishara after midnight, and began to break windows and doors until the police intervened. One Palestinian leader invoked the memory of Kristalnacht in November 1938, which Jews remember as a time when Jewish homes, synagogues, and businesses were attacked.

Only after the lynchings of Arabs had got out of hand were some voices from the peace camp heard: 'What is happening today in Nazareth is a pogrom. It bears all the hallmarks well known to Jews in Tzarist Russia, primarily the collusion between the racist attackers and the police.' Ironically, the largest community in Natsrat Elit, or 'Upper Nazareth,' is of Russian Jews. The daily newspaper, *Haaretz*, in one of the rare editorials recognizing the inherent liability in the dangerous deterioration warned that: 'The severe rioting in Arab locales and at intersections, the shameful incidents of police brutality, which have no justification, and the racist outbursts by Jews in mixed cities – all these have clouded the already fragile relations between Jews and Arabs.'[3]

The Arab minority blamed Barak for the escalation of violence and Israel's reversion to the logic of war – not only vis-à-vis the Palestinians under occupation, but also its 'own' Palestinian minority. The draconian measures taken by the Barak/Ben Ami government fueled a quasi-fascist climate in which Israeli Jews could attack any Arab on sight.

After undertaking its direct attacks on civilians, the government intensified its campaign of arrests, reaching a thousand in the first months. In fact, the police asked Arab hospitals to release the names of all injured Palestinians in order to investigate them after their release. The courts lent a hand to the police as it became evident that the justice system slanted towards the Israeli government, and against the citizens. Even children were kept in custody until their trials were over. The Supreme Court joined in the racist approach of the police and government, rendering the pursuit of justice impossible in Israel. Moreover, the media played a central role in incitement against the Arabs and their representatives, calling them irresponsible, radical, and dangerous, all the while circulating sensationalist reporting on the actions of the Palestinians in Israel.

One Israeli commentator warned of 'a ticking time bomb whose explosion will trigger a civil war.'[4] His sentiment was echoed by Labor Party types – including Nahum Barnea, Dan Margalit, Ehud Ya'ari, and Amnon Abramovitch – who blamed the Arabs. The media was more aggressive regarding the Arab minority than concerning the Palestinians in the Occupied Territories. Television commentator Ya'ari, of Israeli Television Channel One, is a particularly influential war-mongering journalist capable of moving public opinion in Israel.

The failure of the Israeli Left and the 'peace movement' to speak out against the killing of unarmed Arab citizens exercising their civil right to demonstrate has greatly contributed to national polarization between Israeli Arabs and Jews. Its tirades against the Arabs and its defense of the fascist manner in which the government responded to demonstrations spoke volumes about the nature of the Left. Generally, Israelis' reaction to the way their state has treated its Arab citizens underlines a sad fact: while the Labor party was in power, there would be no peace movement capable of standing up to the violations of the civil and human rights of the Palestinian minority, while the ever-needed tolerance would take a back seat to the racist communitarianism of the Jewish majority. Suddenly the Arabs felt very alone and extremely vulnerable in their country.

As a result, the Higher Monitoring Committee, which includes different segments of the population, such as municipalities, NGOs, and political parties, issued a statement demanding international protection from Israeli practices. It sent a letter to UN Secretary General Kofi Annan demanding UN intervention. But unlike their brethren under occupation, the Palestinian citizens of Israel could not muster the same international interest. Half a century of discrimination and confiscation of lands provoked no international indignation. The Israeli Arabs had to take matters into their own hands.

The Palestinian minority's protests and Israel's disproportionate response were summarized by an Israeli commentator as follows:

It is very easy these days to cluck one's tongue and denounce the violence of Israeli Arabs. Throwing stones and smashing streetlights are indeed acts worthy of denunciation. Blocking traffic arteries is improper. Jews on the left and the right are shocked, simply shocked. But who could point to another way available to one-fifth of this country, citizens of the state, after 25 years of discrimination and humiliation? ... It certainly cannot be said that they did not first try nonviolent means. Twenty-five years of exemplary, almost exaggerated loyalty, almost groveling obedience to the state whose wars are not their wars, whose national anthem is not their anthem, whose language is not their language, whose holidays are not their holidays – and for all this it treats them the way it does. Now their youth have started out on the road to violence and it is paying off for them. They know they get nothing without it. Now they are also proving, as their brothers in the territories proved long ago, that Israel the strong achieves nothing through force.[5]

Internal Security Minister Shlomo Ben Ami, who has also served as acting foreign minister, was instrumental in the use of harsh measures to deal with Arab discontent. For more than a year and a half, the only dialogue he conducted with the Palestinian minority was through the threatening loudspeakers of Israeli armored vehicles. The Palestinians have been confronting persistent Israeli land confiscation and blatant discrimination in every area of life. They found no partner for political dialogue with the government. Instead of insuring that such dialogue is established, the Israeli police summoned three Arab Knesset members who represent the majority of the Arabs in Israel – Muhammad Baraka, Abdul Malik Dahamsheh, and Azmi Bishara – in order to investigate allegations of incitement and law-breaking.

Finally, and after much pressure, a state commission was set up to investigate the circumstances that led to the violence. However, the scope of its inquiry was limited to the October events, while the causes of Palestinian anger and the roots of their alienation are embedded in Israeli Zionism and long-standing racism. In the early sessions of the inquiry the commission members heard testimonies from snipers of the Israeli security forces about orders given by their superiors to shoot at unarmed civilians. Moreover, according to the daily *Haaretz*, evidence was provided that buttressed the Arabs' main accusation, namely, that 'Israeli security forces had, without any warning and in an attempt to inflict bodily injuries, used live ammunition alongside rubber bullets.' Furthermore, it emerged in these sessions that the use of live bullets was authorized in the direct instructions issued by the commander of the Israel Police's northern district, Major General Alik Ron.

DECADES OF DISCRIMINATION

Israel's strategy of containment and subjugation of the Palestinian minority has taken different forms over the last five decades – violence, coercion, intimidation, and outright terror – and paralleled its policy in the Occupied Territories. That's how Palestinians became Arab Israelis: with few carrots and many sticks. For many years, Arab municipalities received less than half of the government subsidies Jewish municipalities were handed, while budgetary discrimination in education, health, culture, development, and other areas persisted, and eventually created second-, and even third- and fourth-class citizens in comparison with the Sephardic or Russian immigrants. As a result, one out of every two Arab children in Israel lives below the poverty line, and half of all the children living in poverty are Arabs, even though they represent one fifth of the population, according to figures released by the government in late December 2000.[6]

Barak's Minister of Trade and Industry Ran Cohen admitted that only half of one percent of his ministry's budget goes to the Arabs, who make up some 20 percent of the population, while his ministry employs four Arabs out a total of 540 employees. The same applies to almost all ministries and state companies where the percentage of budget for Arabs, or their employment in the ministries, is a fraction of their percentage in the population. Even in cases where Israel provides certain services, in the words of one Israeli official, 'We take with one hand what we give with the other.'[7] Worse, the discrimination goes beyond budgets and employment.

Years before Israel implemented its policy of colonization and oppression in the West Bank and Gaza, including land confiscation and ethnic cleansing in East Jerusalem following the 1967 war, it had already used those methods of oppression and population control against its own Palestinian minority in the territories it occupied in 1948. Consistently over the last five decades, Israel has confiscated over two-thirds of the land owned by Palestinians inside Israel and on which they depended for their livelihood. Their share of land has dropped from 9 percent to around 3 percent in 2000. They were mostly forced to become laborers in the Jewish Israeli industries and agricultural enterprises. Likewise, when Israel began encircling the Palestinian towns in the West Bank, and Jerusalem, it was already almost halfway through encircling Arab towns and villages in the Galilee, Triangle, and the Negev in Israel proper. In fact, the logic behind Israel's settlement in the West Bank and Gaza was the same as that used in the 'Koening document' (named after the Israeli military governor of the Galilee in the seventies) which was the basis for Judaizing the Galilee where most Arab Israelis reside. The same Zionist, racist, and expansionist logic of encirclement and containment was applied in both cases, especially after ethnic cleansing failed, making little or no difference between territories under occupation and those that are an integral part of the state of Israel.

As time passed, Israeli 'doves' began to reconsider their past treatment of the Arabs. The late Yitzhak Rabin expressed his 'shame' in the early nineties at the way the state treated its Arab minority, and Barak's own chief of staff, Yossi Cucik, apologized recently to Israel's Arab citizens 'for the discrimination against them over the years.' He described the living conditions of the Arabs and Bedouin in Israel and the infrastructure in their towns as 'disgraceful.' However, none of this talk seemed to matter since the discrimination goes beyond budgetary or civil concerns and runs deep in the very colonial nature of the state of Israel and especially its occupation of the West Bank and Gaza. In this context, the Palestinian Israelis are not only second-class citizens, they are also seen as a potential fifth column, and even an internal enemy.[8]

A 'FIFTH COLUMN'

The state of Israel has long considered a fifth of its population to be a potential fifth column. Today, it is clear that it views the Palestinian citizens as the enemy within, even though those Palestinians have proved beyond any reasonable doubt their moderation and their readiness to live in peace and coexistence with Israel's Jewish citizens. In fact, 93 percent of the Arabs voted for Ehud Barak in 1999, and 94 percent voted for Shimon Peres in 1996 and were ready to support any peace initiative that was acceptable to the leadership of both peoples. Moreover, Arab representatives in the Knesset were indispensable in passing a number of crucial peace agreements, including Oslo I and II, opposed by Barak, and Sharm el-Sheikh, signed by him. Nonetheless, as soon as the Israeli Arabs showed solidarity with their brethren under attack in the Occupied Territories, they were equated with the 'subversive minority in Czechoslovakia' that would have turned the Wadi Ara region [in the center of Israel] into a "Middle Eastern Sudetenland".'

In reality, Israel is disturbed by Palestinians of the likes of Azmi Bishara — a candidate for prime minister in 1999 — and Asil Assli, who both reject the undemocratic nature of Israel and refuse to compromise on their basic rights, but take their nationality and their citizenship seriously. Israeli officials and Labor Party leaders have long hoped that the Arabs 'would remain hewers of wood' and, therefore, be easy to control. In fact, they wished the Arabs could all just go away, disappear from Israel's space, memory, and history. During the last five decades, the idea of transferring all the Palestinians has figured strongly in Zionist literature. Until recently, over a third of Israelis wished their state would 'encourage' the Palestinians to leave, and in the context of final status negotiations, some Israelis proposed population exchanges by annexing large blocks of illegal settlements in the West Bank in exchange for relinquishing dense Palestinian areas in the Triangle area to the new Palestinian entity.[9] Soon after the riots began, Haifa University Professor Amnon Sofer proposed to Israeli officials that, in order to solve the demographic problem, they transfer the entire Triangle region to the West Bank in a swap with the settlements that could offload some 250,000 'Arab Israelis' in one stroke.

Almost a third of Israeli Jews support the obliteration of Palestinian citizens' voting rights. Palestinians are tolerated only as long as they confine themselves to a narrow civil agenda and act as a reservoir of votes for Zionist parties. They are expected by the majority to know how to behave as loyal citizens of a state that is not theirs, a state that occupies and wages a daily war on their fellow Palestinians over the hills. However, when they voice their political apprehension about state policy, especially with regard to the occupation, as did happen during the second Intifada, they are considered traitors by over 70 percent of Israelis, and 74 percent reckon Israel would be better off without its Palestinian citizens.[10]

Nonetheless, it is evident today that Israel's goal of sidelining its Palestinian citizens and weakening their will has been turned on its head. The Palestinian minority has come of age five decades after the independence of Israel. The policy of marginalization and depoliticization has produced the opposite: a tendency toward political assertiveness and cultural separation. To Israel's displeasure, the Palestinians who were told to lower their heads and accept their destiny in the Jewish state instead took on the Israeli characteristics of chutzpah and confidence. They demand to live in a liberal democracy that can insure equality and the preservation of their national and cultural identity. To its credit, the Arab minority has begun to produce a new and formidable leadership that can speak the language of justice and democracy beyond the legal rhetoric advanced by Israel, and above the language of fear. They defied conventional wisdom and expectations by succeeding to question the very foundation of the state and propose an alternative multicultural formula that allows Israelis, all Israelis, to coexist, living side by side as equal citizens.

In the recent elections of February 6, 2001, the Arab minority rejected the call of the Labor party and ignored the advice of certain officials in the Palestinian Authority; instead they followed the nationalist call of the National Democratic Assembly, which asked them to boycott the elections. Asked to choose between two hawkish generals more than 85 percent of Palestinians in Israel chose not to vote. This was the first time Israel's Arabs had refused to support the Labor party.

WHAT FUTURE?

Obviously Israel cannot be a democracy for all its citizens while continuing to be an occupying power and a state for all Jews, rather than a state for all its citizens. Israel has proved it can only allow the Palestinians a shadowy existence based on dependency and coercion. For their part, after the second Intifada, the Arabs are more realistic regarding integration and assimilation in the 'Jewish state,' which until now has brought them only marginalization, dependence, and cultural disfigurement. They are all the more keen on achieving equality without integration, until the conditions are ripe for the state to become that of all its citizens, with a new Israeli nationality, the Jews and Arabs of Israel.

Israel has failed to segment and compartmentalize the Palestinian issue, which re-emerged in October as the cause of a whole people, and as the existential challenge facing Israel. It transcends borders and frontiers. This Palestinian minority in Israel has become a central factor in the Israeli-Palestinian equation. In fact, the destiny of the Palestinians in the Occupied Territories and that of Palestinians in Israel has never been as interdependent as it is today.

It is estimated that by 2015, the demographic factor will change in favor of the Palestinians, hence strengthening their demand for equality and liberal democratic norms. In 2000, there are 8.2 million people in historical Palestine, 40 percent of whom are Palestinians, and by the years 2010–2015 it will be fifty/fifty. At the same time, Israeli Arab citizens will comprise a quarter of the country's population, transcending the barriers of small minority into bi-nationalism. In 1999 alone according to Israel's *Statistical Yearbook*, 89,286 infants were born to Jewish mothers, and 34,514 to Moslem mothers, or double their percentage in the population. Moreover, 29,300 Jewish couples were married in Israel, as compared to 17,200 Moslem ones, or more than half. On the other hand, 10,195 couples were divorced last year, and the majority – 9,110 – were Jewish. For the advocates of a Jewish state, this might be a reason to worry. But for those searching for a democratic and enlightened Israel, this is the time to mend bridges with the Palestinians in a spirit of tolerance and equality.[11]

NOTES

1. Israel's mainstream refers to the Palestinian citizens in Israel as 'Israeli Arabs' or 'Israel's Arabs' and the Right likes to refer to them as 'the Arabs of the Land of Israel' or 'Arab Israelis' depending on the context. But in general it's meant to differentiate between them and all other Palestinians, hence, 'Arab' becomes an ethnic or cultural reference rather than Palestinian locus, which might make reference to their right to the land. Worse, and on other occasions, especially in earlier days, Palestinians were referred to by officialdom as 'The sons of the minorities,' i.e. Christians, Moslems and Druze, in addition to other non-Arabs, or in other words in total disregard of their nationality as a minority.

2. The Palestinian Arab minority in Israel is a majority in three regions: Galilee in the north, Triangle in the middle and Naqab in the south of the country. It resides in 8 cities and 47 villages each with over 5,000 inhabitants, 21 of which have a population of over 10,000 Palestinians. Eighty thousand live in mixed cities. Half of the Palestinian population, which comprises about 17 percent of the entire Israeli population, is less than 19 years of age (Israel Central Bureau of Statistics, 1997).

3. *Haaretz*, October 13, 2000.

4. Yoel Marcus, *Haaretz*, October 6, 2000.

5. Gideon Levy, *Haaretz*, October 11, 2000.

6. Ruth Sinai, *Haaretz*, December 20, 2000.

7. Ian Lustick, *Arabs in the Jewish State: Israel's Control of a National Minority*, University of Texas, Austin, 1980, pp. 67–68; *Fasl Al-Maqal Weekly*, February 18, 2000.

8. *Haaretz*, November 3, 2000.

9. Sami Smooha, 'Ethnic Democracy: Israel as an Archetype,' *Israeli Studies* 2, 1997. p. 230.

10. *Middle East International*, October 13, 2000, p. 8.

11. Meron Benvinisti, *Haaretz*, March 26, 1998, and September 13, 2000.

INTERIM

3

IMPASSE IN THE
OSLO DIPLOMATIC PROCESS

If we proved incapable of attaining a coexistence and honest
agreements with the Arabs, then we have understood nothing during
our 2000 years of suffering and we deserve all that will happen to us.
ALBERT EINSTEIN, LETTER TO CHAIM WEIZMAN, NOVEMBER 25, 1929

The starting point for any peace process is the strength and might
of the State of Israel.
EHUD BARAK, AUGUST 13, 1999

As the curtains closed on the last act of the Oslo process at Camp
David II (see p. 46 below), a new chapter was opened in the Israeli-
Palestinian conflict. Israel's harsh and excessive use of force against the
Palestinians since late September 2000, described above in the first two
chapters, has undermined the peace process and, paradoxically, damaged
the security accords, long considered one of Israel's major achievements.

After he had pulled Israeli forces from Lebanon, Ehud Barak
offered the Palestinians two alternatives, but not a realistic choice.
They could either embrace his 'red lines' – notably accepting the
annexation of areas occupied by most of the settlements,
renouncing the Right of Return of the 3.7 million Palestinian
refugees, and surrendering their national and religious symbols in
Jerusalem – or remain under Israeli occupation. The conflict
escalated in response to Barak's arrogant assumption that he could
'end' the conflict through a feckless and humiliating offer.

Naturally, the Palestinians opted for a third alternative: steadfastness. A new popular uprising ensued to send a clear message to Ehud Barak, and a reminder to Yasser Arafat, that they would no longer accept the curtailment of their freedom, threats to their national and religious symbols, or their future held hostage by a stop-go process. If there were any doubt that Arafat could still be pressured into signing an unfair final accord or that Washington, or any other party with clout, could corner him, Palestinian public opinion reflected in the Intifada removed any such illusions.

Soon after the Intifada broke out in response to Likud head Ariel Sharon's provocative visit to Al-Aqsa Mosque and the subsequent killing of six Palestinians in the Haram al-Sharif in Jerusalem, Barak praised Sharon for his merits and contributions to peace. His efforts to join hands with Sharon's Likud Party in a 'national unity government' revealed his war-mongering intentions. Barak went on to convince the Israeli and Western public that Sharon and Likud were good for peace. His recommendations were later conveniently used in Sharon's election campaign. Barak's lavish praise of Likud and 'its historic achievements,' and references to Sharon's contribution to peace confirmed Palestinian and Arab doubts regarding a peaceful end to the conflict. Any such unity government could only be a war cabinet, when there is ostensibly no war. As one mainstream Israeli commentator put it, 'Rumor had it on the Israeli Left that Barak was already voting Likud.' In fact, even after Barak resigned and called for new elections, he continued to entertain the idea of a 'national unity' government with Sharon's Likud.[1]

If the first Intifada of December 1987 had broken out as a result of direct occupation and oppression, the second Intifada was the natural outcome of continued lying, deception, and disappointment over seven long years of what was meant to be peace building and good neighborly relations, referred to as the Oslo peace process. The violence in Jerusalem, Palestine, and in Israel-proper has underlined once again the urgent need to take a critical look at this unfortunate and unjust peace process in order to understand the roots of the Intifada, and, more particularly, the dynamics behind the Palestinians' dissatisfaction. This is necessary to chart a different path for historical reconciliation.

THE PEACE PROCESS: DEFECTIVE DIPLOMACY

The Oslo peace process refers to the last seven years of diplomatic and political efforts to bring Israelis and Palestinians closer, which commenced soon after the end of the Gulf war. This involved, among other things, seven different agreements and various international economic and political summits centered around the 'resolution' of the Palestinian-Israeli conflict, satisfying the demands of both sides.

First there was the Oslo *Declaration of Principles* (DOP), the bedrock of the peace process. It was negotiated in Oslo and signed by Israel and the Palestine Liberation Organization (PLO) in Washington, D.C. on September 13, 1993. The DOP required Israeli recognition of the PLO, withdrawal from the Gaza Strip and Jericho, and additional unspecified withdrawals over an interim five-year period. In exchange, the PLO would recognize Israel and promise to suppress 'terrorism.' The central issues of Jerusalem, water, borders, settlements, refugees, and the future Palestinian entity were reserved for 'final status' talks.

The May 1994 *Cairo Agreement* limited Israeli withdrawal to Jericho and about 60 percent of Gaza, and gave Israel overall security responsibility for internal and external crossings, allowing for the establishment of PNA 'self-rule' over the evacuated territories. The agreement also called for completion of final status talks by May 1999.

The *Taba Agreement* (Oslo II) of September 1995 divided the West Bank into three areas: A, B, and C (see Chapter 1, note 11).

Meanwhile, the *Hebron Protocol* of January 1997 'clarified' the details of Israeli redeployment in Hebron. By this time, the 'functional autonomy' that Israel had ·long desired for the Palestinians, whereby the Palestinians run their own social and municipal services, was now in place. Most Palestinians in crowded cities and refugee camps, generally in areas making up less than a few percent of the total Occupied Territories, were now under their own local authority, leaving the majority of occupied land in Israel's hands. From then on, tough bargaining over the land ensued, turning the peace process into real-estate bickering.

After a lengthy delay, the *Wye River Memorandum* of October 1998, signed by the new Israeli Prime Minister Binyamin Netanyahu, was intended to complete the series of interim arrangements between Israel and the Palestinians prior to the final status negotiations. Its key components included redeployment of Israeli troops from an additional 13.1 percent of the West Bank and an additional Palestinian commitment to Israeli security.

Ehud Barak's *Sharm el-Sheikh Agreement* in 1999 renegotiated clauses in the Wye River agreement, and further toughened security arrangements. It divided the redeployment process into further broken-up stages, but left most other issues untouched. No maps were provided, no figures were released for freeing prisoners, no deadlines were set for the third redeployment which would hand over the rest of the territories to the Palestinians – with the exception of the settlements and military bases. Instead, Barak blocked the implementation of all of the accords and insisted that further redeployment be connected to the final status negotiations. Unfortunately, by force of habit, the Clinton administration went along with it, coercing the Palestinians to come along as well.

Enter *Camp David II*, a summit without preparation, meant to resolve a century-old conflict in a few days at a faraway presidential retreat. Failure was written all over its walls, and yet neither Clinton nor Barak cared to see beyond the strategic void that such failure could create. Israel's proposition of 'all or nothing' meant that if the Palestinians said no to all of Barak's proposals, they would have to remain in the same dire circumstances with no hope of progress and no further redeployment as stipulated in the Oslo agreement. Any such ultimatum was destined to lead either to a breakthrough or an explosion.

CONTEXTUALIZING OSLO

To understand the inherited weaknesses and the subsequent hurdles in the peace process, let us commence from the beginning. Two brief readings are needed for the DOP accords: one textual and the other political, viewing the accords in their regional and historical context. The accords reveal less than they hide. They are vague and wide open to interpretation. But the agreement markedly stipulates that all disputes must be resolved through a Joint Liaison Committee where Israel has a veto power and, hence, the capacity to maintain the status quo, the occupation. Strangely enough, the word 'occupation,' the only legitimate and accurate word to describe Israel's illegitimate presence in the Palestinian territories for some twenty-seven years, was missing from the entire text. Although UNSC Resolution 242 is mentioned as the basis of the negotiations, nowhere is there an admission of occupation. There is also no discussion of the illegal settlements, which, along with the other sensitive and central issues of the conflict – such as the occupation of Jerusalem, the Right of Return of the refugees, and the right of the Palestinians to self-determination – were all postponed and eventually rejected by Israel seven years later.

A political reading of the document shows even bigger problems, notably the continuation of overall Israeli control of the territories, and Israel's ability to manipulate the entire process according to its wishes and needs, especially as the process was doomed to negotiations in stages and implementation in phases. In this case, the powerful party with all the cards, Israel, was able to dictate the pace, spirit, nature, and conclusion of this open-ended process. Moreover, and in the absence of an international legal or institutional authority such as the United Nations, Israeli violations of the Oslo process took place with total impunity, lacking an enforceable arbitration mechanism.

The United States, the only guarantor of the peace process, who could have objected each time Israel violated the agreements, prefered to remain silent. It continued to underline its alliance with Israel, all the while claiming to be an honest broker. Israel began, from the first day, to violate the accords by undermining the 'territorial integrity and continuity of the territories' by planting more settlements, more settlers, and more by-pass roads connecting them, hence compromising the entire process. The same took place in occupied East Jerusalem, but the 'dishonest' broker, the US, covered for its ally Israel. (See Chapter 4 on American policy towards the peace process.)

Soon after the Oslo DOP was signed, a de-politicization of the accords ensued. Israel was able to exploit the fact that the accords were an empty framework, in which each item required another agreement and was open to interpretation – even contradictory ones. The Israeli army, headed by Chief of Staff Barak and General Uzi Dayan, began the process of militarizing the forthcoming interim accords in order to ensure maximum control. This was the underlying principle of the interim Taba agreement, which, among other dangerous elements, divided the West Bank and Gaza into three areas – A, B, and C – instead of only two (see p. 45 above). Hence the accords were rendered hostage to any minor incident that could be used as a pretext to stop their implementation, while also delaying and complicating the transfer of territories to the Palestinians. It also gave Israel a veto power over all economic and political arrangements. By now any major Palestinian move, from the number of Legislative Council members to determining sales tax, was subject to Israeli approval. The appointment of the infamous American CIA as an arbitrator between the two parties further emphasized the importance of security over the political and short-term arrangements in lieu of long-term stability. In the process, sixty-two new military bases were erected in the territories, using American funds, and rendering geographical continuity and, hence, freedom of movement impossible.[2]

In the three years after the inception of the peace process, Israel redeployed from less than 3 (fractured) percent of the land. This represented seven islands of overpopulated towns along with their poverty-stricken refugee camps, deprived of their hinterland, but surrounded by Israeli-controlled areas. The PNA, elected by the

Palestinians of the territories, had to 'govern' within the constrained cluster of Palestinian enclaves. Israel continued its occupation of the remaining 97 percent of the West Bank and 40 percent of Gaza, facilitating the expansion of its settlement drive and the Judaization of Jerusalem, which continued uninterrupted during the Rabin–Peres tenure.

For that purpose, all participants agreed upon items where what Israel was to deliver remained vague and undefined in all the accords, especially in Wye River and Sharm el-Sheik. But when it came to Palestinian obligations, the agreements were detailed to the last pithy item. The Wye River memorandum is almost two-thirds security details, while the central issues of redeployment, final status issues, etc., are only generally dealt with in the remaining one-third, leaving Israel the opportunity to fill the gaps. At the insistence of the Netanyahu government and with America's complicity, such issues as the release of prisoners or the missing maps of the specific areas from which Israel should redeploy were fudged. This allowed Israel to decide unilaterally what areas to redeploy from, and how many criminal prisoners instead of political prisoners to release. In the latest Sharm el-Sheikh agreement, the Barak government reckoned that even Netanyahu's exigency of two-thirds security fell short on certain security requirements and details. Hence, the 'moderate' Barak revisited the security arrangements with America's blessing and praise.

Thereafter, and despite the excitement each time a summit convened and an accord was reached, the situation continued to deteriorate as agreements were violated and more agreements were needed to implement defunct accords. The so-called 'success' of the diplomatic track was not reflective of the socio-economic or political reality on the ground. For seven years, the diplomatic-intensive peace process had overcome ambiguities by merely substituting others. Meanwhile, the implementation of clauses in favor of Israel had negative economic and political effects on conditions in the occupied/autonomous territories and, in fact, led to the deterioration of the standard and quality of living. If the diplomatic theatrics of Oslo succeeded in giving a positive impression in the international media, it was a deceiving lie. Finally, as it ran out of excuses and justifications, the mask fell off and the ugly face of Oslo made itself rudely visible to the disappointment of its proponents. No longer was Uncle Sam capable of pulling more doves from his hat, or magically loosening the knots of Oslo. The magic behind the process faded away as pictures of Israeli tanks, snipers and dead Palestinian children crowded the streets and filled the screens.

CONSTRUCTIVE AMBIGUITY BECOMES DELIBERATE DECEPTION

The impasse in the peace process was predictable for those who viewed it with no illusions. It was a dead-end process because it failed to offer fundamental and legitimate national rights to the Palestinians. But the process survived for three reasons.

First, it rested on the thin line where minimum Palestinian and maximum Israeli demands met. One must recall that when the process began, soon after the end of the Gulf War and the demise of the Eastern Bloc, the PLO was bankrupt and on the verge of collapse, while Israel was reaching a dead end in its negotiations with a weak Palestinian delegation in Washington. In order for it to be allowed into the process and recognized as a 'legitimate' player, the PLO recognized Israel with no specified borders, ignored Israel's settlement drive, gave up the PLO covenant, its armed struggle, and, even if temporarily, abandoned the refugee question – all in exchange for the promise of Gaza and parts of the West Bank. Once the process took off, the Palestinian leadership held its breath while Israel prospered. Since then, it has been hard to detect any overlap between the two.

Second, and at a later stage, the process's survival became more artificial, less responsive, and more dependent on outside coercion and pressure rather than on local satisfaction and progress. 'Thanks' to America's diplomatic clout and international aid, the process continued indefinitely, failing spectacularly. The Palestinians were forced to negotiate new agreements before old ones were implemented. Hence they had to sign Hebron, and later Wye River, before interim agreements were implemented. Later they had to renegotiate Wye River with Ehud Barak before Netanyahu would implement it. This bizarre process of negotiating, renegotiating, and hardly implementing the same aspects of interim agreements, under the wizard diplomacy of Washington, turned the process into a system of population control and Israeli territorial expansion. Meanwhile, the Palestinians, who grew fatally dependent on the American role, were fed false promises and fake guarantees by the Clinton administration.

Third, the process survived on the hope that the final phase would make up for the interim failure. What was referred to in diplomatic lingo as 'constructive ambiguity' in the interim, proved to be 'deceptive ambiguity.' The Palestinians were manipulated into believing that they should take whatever was offered and build on it until the final status negotiations arrived, when they could ask for all their rights. The process that has been mistakenly characterized as 'give and take' meant robbing the Palestinians of their territory with their own 'assent,' while on the other hand, promising to give them 'generously' from what is ultimately theirs. As time passed, the final status requirements seemed to fade away on the Oslo horizon as Jerusalem was encircled, and the West Bank divided by settlements and by-pass roads.

ISRAELI LEADERSHIP CRISIS UNDERMINES DIPLOMACY

The change in Israel's political leadership, from Yitzhak Rabin to Shimon Peres to Binyamin Netanyahu to Ehud Barak, to Ariel Sharon over the last seven years has added to diplomatic instability and the weakening of the accords. But, as Barak's resignation and Sharon's victory have shown once more, the crisis of leadership is embedded in the political system and culture of the state of Israel. The mawkish approach to compromise during periods of calm and the hawkish attitude towards negotiations during turbulent times, make it unlikely that peace will be made without an Israeli de Gaulle, or de Klerk, capable of taking a historic decision to make peace with the Palestinians and stand up, if necessary, to domestic criticism and opposition.

From the beginning, Peres's enthusiasm for Oslo was indispensable in bringing Rabin into the process. But Rabin's assassination by a young, fundamentalist, Sephardic Jew diminished Peres's enthusiasm as he hardened his political position. The murder of Rabin and the background behind his assassination opened a Pandora's box in Israel. Paradoxically, the same camp that had incited his murder won the elections a year later. Rabin's murder was by no means an individual act; it reflected a real crisis in the system and a deep and dangerous polarization in the street. In addition to the atmosphere of hatred and incitement that swept through Israel between 1993 and 1995, it became clear that the radicalization of the Israeli army in the two previous decades played a role in torpedoing the process. The Israeli intelligence agent who incited Yigal Amir to assassinate Rabin was, it seems, a double agent working on behalf of the fundamentalist movement in the security services. Since 1967, Israel's army had been radicalized by the extreme elements that flourished in Israeli society. It is not clear how deep the 'conspiracy' against Rabin went, but it is certainly far from a coincidental act by a lone extremist.

Instead of exploiting the popular anguish toward the assassination and taking the necessary and final steps to push forward a deal with his 'partner,' Yasser Arafat, Peres resorted to his usual opportunism. He became hawkish towards the Palestinians and appeased the National Religious Party (NRP), with whom he conducted coalition negotiations – even though the NRP had organized the street marches against Rabin, depicting him as a traitor. On the other hand, the new Prime Minister Peres, who extended invitations to Jordan's King Hussein and Egyptian President Mubarak to attend Rabin's funeral, did not invite the Palestinian leader, despite the fact that Rabin had died as a result of his handshake with Chairman Arafat. This negative gesture, not Rabin's death, is to my mind the step that ushered in the beginning of the end of the peace process. From then on, it was free fall.

Peres soon opted for violence both in Palestine and in Lebanon, leading to the Qana massacre in Lebanon. Under pressure from the military, he also issued the order to assassinate a Palestinian radical Islamist who was under Palestinian security control, even though at the time Hamas' operations had diminished. Peres's escalation of violence and his bad timing, all under the pretext of fighting terrorism, were met with an escalation of activities by the Islamist movement Hamas. This led to a new circle of violence: a round of suicide operations leading to the deaths of Israeli civilians, further Israeli closures, violence, and other forms of mass punishment against Palestinian civilians. There is certainly no moral equivalence between the piecemeal 'terrorism' of radical groups under occupation, and the wholesale state-sponsored terrorism of Israel in south Lebanon and Palestine.

Naturally, feeling insecure about the entire process, the Israelis elected the radical and populist Netanyahu. Constrained by the Israeli public's new demands for security, he delayed the implementation of the agreements signed by his predecessors with the aim of eventually extinguishing the entire process. Meanwhile, Washington, to keep the process alive, coerced Netanyahu into signing the Wye River agreement which called for additional redeployment from 13 percent of the territories. This, among other reasons, led to his eventual downfall in 1999. The Palestinians, who were coerced into adopting extra measures of oppression and violating the human rights of the Palestinian opposition during the Netanyahu era, once again found themselves short-changed by his successor. Ehud Barak came to power only to demand even greater security guarantees. Worse still, Barak claimed that although the peace process had been conducted on the basis of UN Security Council Resolution 242, the implementation of 242 did not oblige Israel to withdraw to the lines of June 4, 1967, as the Palestinians insist and as the resolution stipulates, because there was never an agreed international boundary between Israel and the West Bank. He also refused to effect any new withdrawals until final status framework agreement was reached.[3] And that was not all.

THE CAMP DAVID CHARADE

As Barak finished his first year, his country's conditions were worsening and his coalition was falling apart. Seventy-seven percent of Israelis said their situation had not improved since Barak took office. Meanwhile, the coalition, based on Barak's decisive electoral victory, soon perished. He invoked the 'civic revolution' and paid lip service to it. Barak hoped that a debate over a liberal constitution permitting, for example, civil marriages, would divide the Right into religious or secular camps. He also anticipated that this constitution would attract the secular bloc toward his government.

But none of Barak's political acrobatics worked. Israel's crisis was deeply rooted in its approach to the peace process. The paralysis in this process seemed to cripple the country politically. Meanwhile, in the absence of progress, the Palestinians intended to declare and realize their state in the Occupied Territories. Israel threatened to retaliate, in the case of a unilateral state declaration, with annexation and violence. Barak refused to move forward with further implementation of agreements, while Clinton, along with his wife Hillary, then a candidate for the New York Senate seat, and his Vice President Al Gore, a candidate for the presidency, were all anxious to have another diplomatic 'victory' in the Middle East. Suddenly all the diplomatic stars were aligned for the convening of a summit – all, alas, but the Palestinians. Enter the Camp David summit.

This was the most deceptive phase of the entire peace process. Barak went to Camp David in order to make the Palestinians accept his ultimatum, an agreement favorable to Israel, or show Israelis and international public opinion that the Palestinian leadership was not ready for peace. At Camp David, Barak had the full support of President Clinton and his advisors, almost all of whom were both Jewish and Zionist. There were no international or legal grounds on which to negotiate. All the Palestinians had was America's 'goodwill,' which, in real terms, translated into one manipulation after another, and one deceptive move on behalf of Israel followed by another. The Palestinians were cornered into accepting unfair 'American bridging proposals,' the same ones the Israelis themselves had proposed in the back corridors, but which had been turned down by the Palestinian leadership. Each time they refused them, the Americans repackaged them, but their substance remained the same. The Palestinians were expected to accept only some parts, but not all, of the West Bank (representing only 22 percent of historical Palestine), while Israel would retain security control over all cross-border movement. (In other words, Palestinians would not be able to leave or enter their own state without Israel's permission.) Palestinians would also have to accept Israel's proposals regarding the 3.7 million refugees, including compensation, residency in the countries in which they took refuge, and immigration to the West, but no Right of Return except for a few thousand, generally the elderly. Finally, the Palestinians were offered a merely nominal authority over Arab East Jerusalem, and control of the Al-Aqsa Mosque area.[4]

Clinton tried to pressure Arafat by offering him an ultimatum on behalf of Israel: recognition of a mini-state in return for giving up on Jerusalem and the refugees and the question of the settlements, a deal that could be buttressed by an aid package to be arranged at the G-7 industrial summit in Okinawa that July weekend. The American plan envisioned postponing the Jerusalem issue for a few more years, if that would make the signing plausible. Arafat refused the American-Israeli 'offer,' and was blamed for refusing to meet Barak 'halfway.' During one of our encounters, Robert Mallet, the American official responsible for the peace process at the White House National Security Council during the Camp David negotiations, criticized the Palestinians for not responding to Israel's suggestions with one of their own in order to keep the process alive. For their part, the Palestinians believed that international legitimacy, not the barter of the Souk, was the basis of the negotiations.

On his return from Japan, Clinton blamed Arafat for not being 'flexible,' like Barak, and threatened him and the Palestinians with isolation, aid cuts, and more. The Palestinians had already gone most of the way to meet Israel, but that was not enough to satisfy Israel's appetite, which seemed to grow with the more Palestinian rights it gobbled up. It was a twisted and distorted solution to the conflict, and one that would not have lasted. It would have put an end neither to the conflict, nor to Palestinian claims. The summit failed and deterioration commenced.

When the moment of truth came at Camp David, Israel handed down its four red lines: no return to the 1967 borders, no dismantling the settlements, no giving back Jerusalem, and no Palestinian sovereignty. It was Barak who spelled out Israel's 'nos', but he reflected the thinking of the Jewish state's political spectrum. There proved to be a national consensus on maintaining control, and on allowing Palestinian independence only within the framework of interdependence, or a Palestinian dependency relationship vis-à-vis Israel.

Barak had summed up his government's diplomatic chapter after Camp David as a 'success.' The prime minister went to Camp David to save himself rather than save the 'peace process.' The result was that 'Israel retained the territories and secured the support of the international community. Presumably, as a successful military commander, Barak looked to expand his freedom of maneuver and leave his "rival" in a dilemma. Barak's military strategy worked, the political process failed and the violence ensued.'[5]

THE LAST-MINUTE NEGOTIATIONS, JANUARY 2001

In the following months, negotiations continued behind the scenes between Palestinians and Israelis, leading to direct official negotiations at the Egyptian resort of Taba in January 2001 from the point they left off at Camp David, and based on bridging ideas presented to them by President Clinton. Those ideas were more forthcoming than the Camp David tactics of President Clinton, especially regarding his recognition of the importance of establishing 'a sovereign, viable, Palestinian state' on all of the Gaza Strip and most of the Occupied Territories. Clinton also proposed that Jerusalem should 'encompass the internationally recognized capitals of two states, Israel and Palestine.' He recommended a partitioned sovereignty in East Jerusalem where what is Jewish would become Israeli and what is Arab would become Palestinian in order to allow for an 'undivided' and 'open city.' He proposed the return of the refugees to the Palestinian state. All these recommendations proved the Palestinians were right to say 'no' to Clinton at Camp David and that there was more room for American maneuver and Israeli compromise. Nonetheless, Clinton made his ideas known only thirteen days before leaving office and less than a month before the Israeli elections.

The PLO leadership felt that Clinton's disregard of the Palestinian Right of Return to areas they had come from inside Israel and his insistence that all major Israeli settlements, including those in East Jerusalem (Palestinian) neighborhoods, be annexed to Israel, would be unacceptable to most Palestinians. Insisting that the Palestinian state 'accommodates Israel's security requirements and demographic realities' would, in fact, split the putative Palestinian state into three bantustans in the West Bank, with militarily-reinforced settlements in between (see maps).

The Palestinians could not afford to say no to Clinton and risk diplomatic isolation. They opted for a strictly conditional acceptance. Barak, on the other hand, could not risk appearing a moderate during the elections, so responded very conditionally as well. The negotiations yielded a more extensive Israeli withdrawal from the Occupied Territories, but involved tighter Israeli security conditions. They enforced the underlying Israeli correlation between the Palestinian territories and sovereignty: the less Israel yielded on the land, the more generous it stood on Palestinian sovereignty, and the more land it gave up to the Palestinians in the negotiations, the less sovereignty it allowed them. In other words, Israel was ready to grant the Palestinians complete sovereignty in the Gaza strip, but only an expanded *autonomy* on 90 percent of the West Bank, which eventually would have certain characteristics of sovereignty, like the South African homelands. Otherwise, the Palestinians could expect half a state on half of the West Bank.

Nonetheless, the Taba negotiations did make a dent in the Israeli position, but it was too little too late. Clinton was out, Barak was down in the polls, and Sharon's victory was all but secured. The Palestinians untangled their national calendar from the Israeli and American elections and opted to take the risk of time. Barak went down taking the Oslo process with him, signaling the opening of a new chapter in the Palestinian-Israeli conflict.

SHARON'S VICTORY

Sharon's victory, with some 60 percent of the vote, meant that any meaningful initiative to bridge the gap between Palestinians and Israelis ceased. In the months following his election all attempts to reach a compromise with the Palestinians were blocked. In May, after five months' investigation and in an attempt to facilitate the return to the negotiating table, the international American-led commission recommended that both parties cease hostilities and that Israel impose a complete freeze on the settlements, including on any so-called 'natural growth.'

This recommmendation was also underlined in the Egyptian-Jordanian peace initiative launched a few weeks earlier to facilitate a return to the negotiations. Palestinian leader Yasser Arafat accepted both sets of recommendations. So did the majority of Israelis, according to Israel's daily *Yediot Ahronot*. But not their general/premier, Ariel Sharon. He rejected any halt to settlement activity, proposing instead an additional $400 million for further expansion.

Sharon's answer to the Palestinian uprising has been to order the use of more Israeli fire-power and a tightening of the closures. Since the ongoing siege of Palestinian areas began 'there has been no reduction in the number of violent incidents − quite the contrary,' according to Israel's leading daily, *Haaretz*, the violence had become more widespread and more serious. In fact, "collective punishment lacks even a pretense of having a security purpose", according to *Haaretz*.

Israel's premier missed the basic lesson in Palestine, that war, contrary to the Clausewitz doctrine, is not diplomacy by other means. Incapable of or rather unwilling to reach a historic compromise with the Palestinians along the lines of the 1967 borders, the Sharon government continued the same logic of violence that has so far yielded little to Israel and done much damage to the chances of coexistence and peace.

Fifty years after its independence, Israel has missed its chance of being accepted as a member of the community of states in the Middle East. Instead of finally taking the opportunity for recognition on some 78 percent of historical Palestine by all its Arab neighbors, Sharon claimed that his country was still fighting its war of independence. A complete triumph of Zionism would have been possible through a reconciliation process with the Palestinian 'neighbors.' And so, an unrelenting Israel took the region into another cycle of instability and violence.

NOTES

1. Hemi Shalev, *Maariv*, October 27, 2000.
2. Edward Said, *The End of the Peace Process*, Pantheon Press, New York, 2000, p. 25.
3. Aluf Benn, *Haaretz*, July 5, 2000.
4. Akram Haniyeh, *The Camp David Papers*, 2000, Al-Ayam, Ramallah, p. 43.
5. Aluf Ben, *Haaretz*, September 12, 2000.

4

THE REAL ROLE OF THE UNITED STATES IN THE PEACE PROCESS

Aid to Israel on a historically unprecedented scale, in practice without strings attached, permitted Israel to rebuff various regional peace initiatives proposed by Washington and use American-supplied arms in disregard of the officially imposed restraints.

GEORGE LENCZOWSKI, *AMERICAN PRESIDENTS AND THE MIDDLE EAST* (DUKE UNIVERSITY PRESS, DURHAM NC, 1990, p. 282)

When Anwar Sadat went to Camp David, the American team included one Zionist Jewish official, American Ambassador to Israel Samuel Lewis. When Arafat went to Camp David, all the American team, with the exception of President Clinton, were Zionist Jews. Instead of meeting Democrats and Republicans, the Palestinians, like the Syrians before them, met Likudnik and Laborite American officials.

ARAB COMMENTATOR

Since the American-sponsored 'peace process' between Arabs and Israelis was launched, soon after the end of the Gulf war nine years ago, it has become a dominant factor in shaping the Middle East's daily reality. At the outset, an international conference for peace in the Middle East was convened in Madrid in 1991 to show that the new-found international will to act against aggression in the post-Cold War era was truly international, and far from selective in its application of the principles of international legality long blocked by East–West hostilities. We were told that this will to act would go beyond punishing Iraq for its invasion of Kuwait, and would rid the region of all forms of occupation and conflict – notably Israeli occupation of Arab land – to achieve peace and stability. Instead, a victorious Washington began to transform inter-regional relations to suit American priorities and Israel's interests. Israeli economic hegemony coupled with military superiority vis-à-vis an economically dependent, unstable, and insecure Palestine, was cemented in formal accords sponsored by Washington.[1]

US policy toward the peace process has varied in style, but has been consistent since its inception. In order to keep a steady course in the frequently stormy waters of the Middle East, the American role changed at different junctures in the negotiations. It swung from a mere facilitator, hosting the concerned parties, to a 'full partner,' writing compromises and imposing them on the junior partners. Overall, it became the political and diplomatic presence that drafted compromises and wrote letters of guarantees to the parties. Soon America became the judge, the jury, and the prosecutor all in one.

Washington holds primary responsibility for the failure of the Oslo process because its appeasement of Israel and disregard for international legality were destined to lead to failure. Its primary emphasis on a security approach was to its detriment. Once protests broke out against the unfair peace process and Israel used American-made helicopters, gunships, tanks, and armored vehicles to quell Palestinian demonstrators and attack Palestinian neighborhoods, US Secretary of State Madeleine Albright urged 'restraint' and praised Barak's 'commitment to peace,' while demanding that Arafat 'stop the stone throwing and violence.' Alas, the lesson had not been learned.

US CONSIDERATIONS, US GOALS

Four factors have characterized the American diplomatic effort since the signing of the Oslo accords on the White House lawn on

September 13, 1993. First, its ideological-strategic relations with Israel; second, internal political pressure, especially from the Israeli lobby, the most renowned lobby for its capacity to promote, damage, or block the political careers of presidents and congressmen; third, the preoccupation with establishing an American-dominated zone of trade and security cooperation in the Eastern Mediterranean with the participation of Turkey; and fourth, insuring that the international community, American domestic legal authorities and the UN are kept out of the process of conflict resolution.

All four guidelines revolved around Israel and, hence, six principles had to be respected at all times during the negotiations in order to guarantee the continuity of the process:

1. Insure Israel's internal stability and political and economic well-being, hence offering full and unconditional support to the Rabin, Peres, and Barak governments, and legitimizing the Netanyahu and Sharon governments, even when the latter expressed its hostility towards the process.
2. Accept Israeli security arguments without reservations under the justification that Israel knows its security better than anybody else.
3. Maintain Israeli military superiority over all other countries in the region combined.
4. Perpetuate the military and legal asymmetry between Israel and the Palestinians in order to keep the latter dependent on the Israelis.
5. Suggest a moral asymmetry between Israel and the Palestinians to the advantage of the 'democratic' and 'generous' Zionist state whose surplus morality stands in contrast with 'ungracious' and 'ungrateful' Palestinians.
6. Insure that all moves and initiatives in the process are coordinated with Israel before they are put on the table.

In this context, America was in no way, shape or form an 'honest broker' or a 'peace maker' in the region, as the astonished

Palestinians had discovered at Camp David. It was coercive in its approach, and imperialist in its vision. America's outrageous tilt toward its Israeli ally was further demonstrated in the way the Clinton team, mostly Zionist Jews who acted on behalf of Israel's Left and Right, repeatedly presented Israeli proposals to the Palestinians as 'American bridging proposals,' (even though Arafat told Clinton that he had already received these very proposals through confidential channels from the Barak government). When the Palestinians rejected them, Washington complained that they were not abiding by the text and spirit of international legality.

In contrast, America vowed to support Israel if it took the necessary 'risks' for peace, and promised to remain on its side if it thought those 'risks' were too great. Alas, the risks were always 'great' and only Israel can assess its risks. In other words, Israel was immune from any pressures if it refused to implement the agreements or violated UN resolutions that have been the basis of the negotiations, notably UN Resolution 242 calling for the exchange of land for peace.

This was complemented by economic conferences that paved the way for further liberalization, privatization, and open markets. In this spirit of a new Near East Pax-Americana, Washington supported Israel with more generous military and economic aid, and subsidized the Palestine National Authority's security in order to contain the repercussions of the inherently unstable and unjust 'peace process.'

In order to maintain its intermediary act, the Clinton administration used a number of deceitful methods that had become salient characteristics of its diplomacy. In plain English: the Clinton administration consistently lied to the Palestinians and deceived their leadership into believing it understood and sympathized with their frustration and anxiety as the terms of reference shifted and narrowed, especially when UN resolutions were being by-passed or blatantly violated.

Attaching letters of guarantees, or 'letters of assurances,' to the worked-out draft agreements for the parties to sign has been one of the more frequent actions taken by US governments. The assurances regarding the settlements and Jerusalem underlined the deceit of the American administration. Letters of assurances, which were handed out to the parties to calm their suspicions, were instrumental in keeping the process intact. The first Bush administration, and later the Clinton administration, threatened those who did not accept the letters of assurances with severed relations and alienation. But they also offered incentives to abiding states, including grants, loans, arms, and an audience with the president of the United States. It was the well-known carrot-and-stick policy. In fact, during his tenure at the White House, President Clinton met with Chairman Arafat more than with any other foreign leader, according to one National Security Council insider. Clinton became intimate and even passionate about the peace process, but the pro-Israeli guidelines he pursued led to peace regress (see chapters on Jerusalem and the settlements).

COERCIVE DIPLOMACY

Using carrots for Israel and mostly sticks on the Palestinians, Washington's approach to 'peace' has been based on security and military measures as guarantors of peace, instead of the opposite – peace as the ultimate source of security. America adopted Israel's position of demanding a peace agreement in order to effect a partial pull-out, instead of using the pull-out to pave the way for a final agreement after thirty-three years of occupation. For seven years it stressed the importance of security regimes, bilateral security arrangements, systematic security coordination, and preventive security measures.

Using the Oslo peace process and its derivative accords – whether from Cairo, Taba, Hebron, Wye River, or Sharm el-Sheikh – the CIA began to play a terrestrial security role and America became involved in implementing the security clauses of the Oslo accords.[2] The CIA participated in bilateral and trilateral biweekly meetings with Palestinian and Israeli security representatives. This was in addition to overseeing the forensic cooperation and preventive security measures taken by the Palestinians against the infrastructure of those who oppose the peace process. In fact, CIA personnel became part of the power structure in the Gaza Strip, where the Palestinian security headquarters is located. Moreover, nine Palestinian security organs were functioning with budgets and structures and in coordination with Israel during the Oslo process.

Final status negotiations ensued soon after the interim process was implemented in Israel's favour. Washington began consultations with Israeli officials on a military aid package which could cost American taxpayers some $17 billion. This was considered an inducement for Israel to sign peace agreements with Syria and the Palestinians, involving withdrawals from the Golan and the West Bank. Washington proposed to Israel a strategic defense pact, the sort which had only ever been signed with NATO countries, Japan, and South Korea after the Second World War.[3]

AMERICA CAVES IN ON THE ILLEGAL SETTLEMENTS

Over the last three decades, America's position on settlement in the Occupied Territories was turned on its head, to the detriment of the peace efforts. In the late 1960s, the US official line maintained that the Fourth Geneva Convention applied to the Occupied Territories. In the 1980s, President Ronald Reagan said publicly that he did not think settlements were illegal, thereby signaling a new, softer US stance. Thereafter, the US still opposed settlements as 'an obstacle to peace.' US policy stiffened again when President George Bush attempted to renew the peace process in 1990 after the Gulf war. Secretary of State James Baker was furious when Israeli Prime Minister Yitzhak Shamir repeatedly greeted his frequent shuttles to Israel by announcing new settlements.

The US letter of assurances of October 18, 1991 to the Palestinians stipulated that:

The United States has long believed that no party should take unilateral actions that seek to predetermine issues that can only be resolved through negotiations. In this regard the United States has opposed and will continue to oppose settlement activity in the territories occupied in 1967, which remains an obstacle to peace ... Thus, we do not recognize Israel's annexation of East Jerusalem or the extension of its municipal boundaries, and we encourage all sides to avoid unilateral acts that would exacerbate local tensions or make negotiations more difficult or pre-empt their final outcome.

Eight years later and in another letter of assurances dated September 4, 1999, this time from Secretary of State Madeleine Albright, it was stipulated that: 'Fourth, we are conscious of your concerns about settlement activity. As President Clinton has written to you in the past, the United States knows how destructive settlement activity has been to the pursuit of Palestinian-Israeli peace.'

In the period between these two letters of assurances, Israeli settlement efforts multiplied, at times indirectly using funds from American aid to Israel. Moreover, no specific mention of Jerusalem was made in Secretary of State Madeleine Albright's 1999 letter of assurances, although Washington was well aware of the fact that the Barak government had finished the first phase of building in the 'Abu Ghnaim' Palestinian neighborhood of Jerusalem, renamed Har Homa by the Israelis.

By contrast, in July 1969, two years after the 1967 war had ended with the Israeli occupation of East Jerusalem, US Representative to the UN Security Council Yost had rejected any settlement in East Jerusalem, claiming that the Fourth Geneva Convention on Occupied Territories applied in the case of East Jerusalem, and hence the occupied city must be left intact until a resolution was found. He claimed that Washington continued to reject any changes in the city. Thirty-two years later, the Clinton administration refused to treat these territories as Occupied Territories. They have become merely 'disputed' territories. Never has the subject of Jerusalem been so slanted and contradictory to international legality and justice as during the Clinton tenure. In fact, the Clinton administration decided to move its embassy from Tel Aviv to Jerusalem, where it accepted a plot of land donated by Israel, even though it had been confiscated from its Arab owners – ninety of whom are today American citizens, according to Palestinian historian Walid Khalidi.

The Clinton administration ignored the settlement issue and referred to it merely as 'unhelpful,' dropping the former 'obstacles to peace' since it was continuing its 'peace' efforts while settlement was going on. By March 1993, in his testimony before Congress, Assistant Secretary of State for the Middle East Edward Djerejian maintained that 'there is some allowance for – I wouldn't use the word expansion but certainly continuing some activity – construction activities in existing settlements.' More importantly, on October 4, 1994, after the signing of the Oslo agreement, Assistant Secretary of State for the Middle East Robert Pelletreau stated to Congress that:

1. Settlement expansion, after the Oslo agreement, was no longer an 'obstacle to peace' but merely a 'complicating factor in the peace process.'
2. Settlement expansion is not inconsistent with the Declaration of Principles.
3. Privately-funded settlement construction does not violate any agreement with the US.
4. Settlement expansion in Jerusalem is not considered by the US to be a unilateral action prejudicial to determining the final status negotiations.

A year later, US Ambassador-designate to Israel Martin Indyk, who came to the administration from the ranks of the Israeli lobby in Washington, explained to the Senate Foreign Relations Committee that settlement may complicate the peace process, but that other issues such as terrorism are more complicating by far. Hence, the US should concentrate its diplomatic efforts on such dangers rather than on the settlement issue. And in 1997, Secretary of State Madeleine Albright called simply for a 'time-out' on settlement building – a position so weak as to effectively strip American disapproval of any substance. In April 1999, the State Department admitted through its spokesman that Israel had violated its commitment to the US regarding settlements, but downplayed the fact.[4]

America's contribution to Israel's increasing presence in the Occupied Territories makes the US as responsible for the situation as Israel. Helping countries to violate international law and to institute a system of national discrimination and Apartheid is an infraction of that law. The US has supported UN Resolution 446, which specifically requires Israel to unconditionally withdraw from the settlements, while UN Resolution 465 forbids any country to support Israel's colonization drive. On the one hand, the American Congress demanded that the administration deduct whatever Israel spends on settlements from the $2 billion annual installment of the $10 billion loan provided to Israel in 1992. But on the other hand, America's annual aid of well over $3 billion to the Jewish state continues to subsidize the settlement drive and the military bases that guard them. Special American Coordinator of the Peace Process Dennis Ross promised the Israeli government that his administration would find ways to restore its full funding. This was the same Ross who, in February 1999, characterized the settlements as the most serious danger threatening the peace process at the time; but his declarations, like those of his predecessors, were not accompanied by any US action.[5]

PALESTINIAN AND ISRAELI PERCEPTIONS OF AMERICA'S ROLE

Like President Sadat before him, Arafat considered the solution to the conflict to be in America's hands. Sadat had believed that '99 percent of the cards' to solve the conflict and recuperate Egyptian lands were in Washington's hands, an erroneous perception that was then used by Washington to impose a deal on Egypt at Camp David I in September 1978. This method was also repeated at Camp David

II with the Palestinians in July 2000. Arafat erroneously believed that Clinton was the only politician capable of saving him from Israel's violence, both in the negotiations and on the ground. This translated into more compromises to insure Washington's successful diplomacy and to ameliorate Arafat's relations with the United States. Arafat became a regular visitor to the White House and Clinton could count on him when the peace process was stuck. Arafat's compromises were converted into essential fuel for the continuation of the negotiations, and Washington's role became the necessary lubricant keeping the peace industry alive.[6]

On another level, the Palestinians, like their fellow Arabs, familiarized themselves with the individual politicians rather than studying the institutional background they represented. Hence, they trusted the likes of Shimon Peres and Yitzhak Rabin, and trusted that Barak would deliver. The Palestinians also trusted Clinton and were charmed by his performance, just as the late Anwar Sadat trusted Henry Kissinger in the late seventies. This 'personal' approach paved the way for Washington and the Israelis to extract many compromises from the Palestinians, who were asked to put their faith in Rabin, who was assassinated, and in Peres and Barak, who were defeated, and later to put their faith in Clinton, who manipulated them and moved on.

Israelis for their part, were wary of too much American involvement in the negotiations. In spite of America's obvious tilt toward Israel, the leaders of the Jewish state were careful not to mix the priorities and visions of a superpower with their own, since at times they weren't necessarily compatible. Israelis thought too much American involvement would lead to pressure on Israel, even if it were a minor pressure. This was the case for the Begin government during the Camp David accords – as was confirmed by Begin's ministers Moshe Dayan and Ezer Weizeman – and this was what transpired in the American involvement during the Shamir and the Netanyahu governments.

Moreover, like Rabin before him, Barak understood the importance of keeping Washington engaged but deterring it from imposing an alternative agenda of its own – as it was disposed to do in the case of the Rogers plan, Carter's International Conference, the Reagan plan, the Madrid International Conference, or the Wye River compromise. In the latter, Netanyahu objected to the American compromise of Israeli redeployment in 13.1 percent of the territories, halfway between what the Palestinians asked and what the Israelis proposed. Initially, Barak wanted to keep America on the sidelines, but once Washington insisted on getting involved, after the negotiations passed through rocky times, he only accepted on the condition that its moves be coordinated with Israel in advance.

BLACKMAILING THE PALESTINIANS

America has repeatedly used everything at its disposal to pressure the Palestinians into compromise. For example, it used the Syrian card to exploit the bad relations between Arafat and the late President Hafez al-Assad. At the beginning of 1999, Syrian-Israeli negotiations took a leap forward when Syrian Foreign Minister Farouq As-Shara met with Prime Minister Ehud Barak in Washington to discuss conditions for withdrawal, security arrangements, and normalization of relations. The Palestinians felt cornered by the development, particularly after hearing As-Shara's speech on the White House lawn stating that, once an agreement was reached with Syria based on full withdrawal from Syrian and Lebanese territories, Israel could expect to normalize its relations with the region. The Syrian official did not mention the outstanding Palestinian grievances or Israeli withdrawal from the Occupied Territories, a matter that further worried the Palestinians. And so, the Palestinians went back to the negotiating table and accepted what they had earlier rejected: the Israeli maps dictated to them by the Netanyahu government detailing the third stage of the second redeployment. In December 1999, just as the Palestinians announced that they were freezing all negotiations until the issue of the settlements was resolved with the Barak government, Secretary Albright suddenly announced that she was optimistic after her visit to Syria. This was simply another maneuver to pressure the Palestinians into accepting the settlement issue.

The US, and particularly the Congress, has also used its domestic agenda as an instrument of pressure on the Palestinians. The Clinton administration, presumably a friend, demanded Arafat's help in co-opting a radical Congress by making more compromises and less trouble. Although the PLO is the legitimate representative of the Palestinian people and a full partner in the peace process, its offices in Washington continue to function conditionally on the Congress's approval every six months. Only after strong recommendations from the White House that the Palestinians have complied with American guidelines on security issues did Congress allow Washington to maintain normal diplomatic relations with the PLO.

This was also the case regarding the Congressional threat to move the American embassy to Jerusalem by the end of 1999. The implementation was repeatedly postponed in return for Palestinian compromises to keep the process alive. The threat to move the embassy was explicitly used during Camp David. Moreover all major aid packages that must be approved by Congress, where the Israeli lobby has been incredibly influential, has translated into more American pressure on the Arab partners to come forward with convincing proof of their loyalty and sincerity towards the peace process as seen by Israel.

FAILURE: FROM CLINTON TO BUSH

The peace process has largely been characterized by America's overall security-oriented policy in the Middle East. Moreover, Israeli security needs, national and individual, in Israel as well as in the illegal settlements, were seen as the pillar of any future arrangements, even if that was achieved at the expense of the Palestinians and at the risk of compromising the sovereignty of their future state. In fact, America's policy transformed the process into a continuous, even permanent, ceasefire rather than a peace agreement. Once the ceasefire collapsed on September 28, 2000,

Washington blamed the Palestinians, when it had only itself to blame. It wasted one opportunity after another to broker a peace settlement guaranteeing minimum Palestinian national rights as well as the security and coexistence of Palestine and Israel as equal states.

The Clinton administration proved to be one of the most pro-Israeli administrations for five decades. In fact, it was the worst, both in terms of its lack of commitment to international legality and traditional official American positions regarding the illegal settlements, Jerusalem and the refugees. In spite of giving the Palestinians assurances to the contrary, the Clinton administration changed Washington's position on settlement in the West Bank and the annexation of East Jerusalem from one that viewed both as destructive to or at least obstacles in the way of the peace process, to accepting them as *faits accomplis*.

The Clinton team ignored the central issues of contention where solutions could bring stability, in favor of security relations, security preoccupations, and security measures. In Palestine itself, the 'security logic' of the peace process and America's exigency in underlining the logic of force has already been transformed into an authoritative 'logic of force' in the Palestinian entity.

Erroneously equating the peace process with peace, America succeeded in hailing itself as peacemaker and Israel as senior peace partner, even when it was violating international law. Hence Israel's impunity in international circles was totally assured by Washington, which naturally encouraged Israel to continue its violations of Palestinians' rights. In fact, the American-sponsored peace process provided the necessary cover for Israel to expropriate more lands, encircle the Palestinians in their townships, dominate them economically, and control them physically. When the Intifada finally put an end to the charade, the United States was embarassed in its role as Israel's protector by scenes like the notorious picture of a frightened Palestinian child facing his death at the hands of an Israeli soldier.

The election of George W. Bush brought with it ill-placed optimism among some that Washington would distance itself to some extent from Israel under the new administration. Wrong again. The Clinton administration had tried to separate the Gulf crisis, and particularly Iraq, from the area of Palestine–Israel, the two hot spots in the Middle East. It articulated two separate policies to deal with each: containment for the northern Gulf and the peace process for the Near East. The Bush administration announced that it would look at the region as a whole and view the Palestinian–Israeli question in this dimension. It would also consider any show of solidarity with Iraq by the Palestinians as an unfriendly gesture toward the United States. The Bush administration could be different from the Clinton administration in style and approach, but in the final analysis, it will not be any less pro-Israel.

NOTES

1. America – itself once called 'the new Israel' – which conducted ethnic cleansing on a large scale in the other 'promised land,' identified with the colonial behavior of industrious Israel that succeeded where it had failed in the third world, notably to crush the Arab armies in 1967 when America was failing in Vietnam. Overall, America's diplomacy in the Middle East has been built on security measures, military operations, and power relations. In the Gulf region, America secured its dominance over the West's energy supplies through a policy of war, containment, blockade, intimidation, subversion, and preventive military actions. In the Near East it secured Israel's superiority over all its Arab neighbors and supported its war efforts against 'unfriendly' nationalist Arab regimes.

2. America's emphasis on security arrangement can be traced to the days of Henry Kissinger, who asked Israeli prime ministers Eshkol, Meir, and Rabin not to settle for peace accords but to demand strict security measures that the United States could supervise.

3. For its part, the Barak government requested a one-way version of the pact committing America to protect Israel, but not putting limits on its military operations. Barak preferred to upgrade Israel's strategic

relations with the United States, which would give it more security guarantees and military aid that could continue to insure its long-term superiority over its Arab neighbors (Aluf Ben, *Haaretz*, April 7, 2000).

4. Geoffrey Aronson, 'US policy and the impact of settlement on the peace process,' in *Settlements and Peace: The Problem of Jewish Colonization in Palestine*, Center for Policy Analysis on Palestine, Washington DC, 1995, pp. 17–18.

5. Stephen Zunes, 'The strategic functions of US aid to Israel,' *Middle East Policy*, Vol. 4, No. 4, October 1996, p. 95.

6. Shibley Telhami, 'From Camp David to Wye: changing assumptions in Arab-Israeli negotiations,' *The Middle East Journal*, Vol. 53, No. 3, Summer 1999. pp. 380–382.

FINAL STATUS NEGOTIATIONS

5

THE PALESTINIAN REFUGEES

We shall drive them out and take their place.
BEN GURION IN A LETTER TO HIS SON IN 1937

In 1948 we expelled them, or else they left as a result of the war.
EHUD BARAK, *HAARETZ*, NOVEMBER 29, 2000

THE MOST IMPORTANT 'FINAL STATUS' ISSUE

The refugee issue is the most important of all so-called 'final status issues.' Nonetheless, it was marginalized and ignored during the negotiations. For Israel the issue of the refugees remained a taboo, although it was listed as one of the issues that Israelis and Palestinians needed to agree upon. Today, 3.7 million registered refugees remain outcast after being driven from their houses and country, mostly under war conditions. Of these, 1.2 million continue to live in some sixty camps after fifty years of exile. In fact, the majority of Yasser Arafat's Gaza constituency, or 729,000, are refugees; almost 600,000 more are in the West Bank, and the majority of the rest live in Lebanon (400,000), Syria (460,000), Jordan (almost one third of all refugees), and other Arab countries.

The Palestinian refugee issue symbolizes the Palestinian problem. It has been at the root of the Israeli-Palestinian and Israeli-Arab conflicts since 1948, when 85 percent of the Palestinian Arabs living on 82 percent of the land, of what is today Israel, were driven out of their homes by the Zionist forces and have not been allowed back since. This expulsion ushered in a new era that lies at the root of an Israeli-created Apartheid. As in South Africa, where the blacks, who made up 67 percent of the population, could not set foot in 92.3 percent of the land, so did the new state of Israel exclude three-quarters of the original inhabitants from their land, forbidding them to return.

The Palestine Liberation Organization (PLO) was established by the refugees and was nourished and supported over the years by their sacrifices in aspiring to freedom, shelter and return to their homeland. This is the only issue that links the 1967 and 1948 wars, and therefore dealing with it is a precondition to reaching any final agreement between Israelis and Palestinians that will address the roots of the conflict. Nonetheless, Israel has refused to address this question for five decades, and when it finally had to confront it at the Camp David summit in July 2000, it blamed the Arabs for it and denied any moral, political, or legal responsibility. Instead, it warned that it did not recognize the Right of Return of these refugees. After a short and superficial discussion at the summit, Israel agreed to allow a few thousand to return over a ten-year period based on humanitarian need, and agreed to support an international fund that would compensate the refugees.

In reality, the question of the refugees and the 1948 war, unlike the 1967 war and occupation, comprises an existential question for Israel, one that obligates an admission of its original crime, and a recognition of responsibility for its actions, but which it chooses to ignore and even erase from its memory and its history books. Massacres, terrorism, forced evacuation, house demolitions, and an all-out campaign of ethnic cleansing that destroyed some 400 Palestinian villages, have all been denied by Israeli official delegations, although the books of its new historians and newly released documents are saturated with details about the ethnic cleansing that the Zionists carried out in Palestine. True, Oslo came on the basis of UN Resolution 242, which deals primarily with the results of the 1967 war. But the only way to reach a definitive agreement is by addressing the question of the refugees as one of the final status issues at the negotiations, refering to UN Resolution 194 calling for the Right of Return, which has been affirmed a hundred times over the last fifty years since the 1948 war. The Right of Return has been classified by the UN as an 'inalienable right.'

THE REFUGEE QUESTION IN THE NEGOTIATIONS

While negotiators at Camp David II were busy trying to find a minimum agreement, and the American delegation was trying to formulate bridging ideas for a framework agreement, Ehud Barak dismissed UN Resolution 194, which affirms the international position on the rights of the Palestinian refugees. This was considered a mistake by the legal adviser to the Israeli delegation, Elyakim Rubinstein, who advised Barak instead to insist on inserting UN General Assembly Resolution 194 by name in order for the agreement to cover all the Palestinian claims without necessarily satisfying them. The agreement was to end with the assertion that, with the signing of the document, the Palestinians would have no further claims in Israel; the agreement would then become the presumed compensation for the refugees and a satisfactory implementation of UNGA 194.

But how could the PLO, the product of the refugee environment, agree to sign away all claims when Israel refused to admit moral or political responsibility for the refugees' misfortune? Israel's answer came on two levels. First, the Jewish state was not responsible for what had happened. It was rather the Arab armies who had attacked the young state and told the Palestinians to leave their homes until such time as an Arab military victory allowed them back. No record of such an exhortation was ever found. Second, Israel claims that the PLO had already accepted Israel's position on the Right of Return principle when it agreed to UN Resolution 242 as the basis for negotiation, a resolution that addresses only the 1967 war and its aftermath and does not refer to the 1948 war. The

Palestinians affirm that only the transitional process was based on 242, otherwise why would the issue be mentioned at all as a final status issue? Purely for humanitarian reasons, according to the Israelis.

The rebuttal goes on regarding the legal, political, and other aspects of finding a solution to the Palestinian and Israeli claims, but the basic principles remain the same regardless of who is right or who is wrong: the refugee question cannot be ignored. This is especially true when the alternative is considered, i.e. accepting ethnic cleansing and granting Israel the right to prevent the original inhabitants of the country from returning to their homes. Even if the Palestinians had left of their own accord, as the Israelis claim, international law stipulates that, regardless of the causes of conflict, civilians have the right to return to their homes. The Israelis claim that the Right of Return will amount to the end of the Jewish state. But, in fact, today 78 percent of the Jewish population lives in 15 percent of Israel's lands, and most of the remaining Israeli Jews live in about two dozen urban centers which were in the main originally Palestinian. This leaves 154,000 Israelis in control of a relatively big territory of 17,000 sq. km., mostly expropriated from the 4.9 million refugees (registered and non-registered with UNRWA). If the Gaza refugees were settled in the southern part of the country where most of them came from originally, and the refugees from Lebanon were allowed to settle in the Galilee whence they originated, it would change little the demographics of the Jewish majority in the areas they inhabit.[1] Neither would it change the demographics of the country as a whole.

Israel, one must remember, agreed to Resolution 194 when it joined the UN in 1949. In fact, that same year Israel agreed to the return of 100,000 refugees after American President Harry Truman asked that 300,000 be allowed to return to their homes. But soon after its admission to the international organization, Israel reneged on its position while the international community looked the other way. Although the UN had set up the UN Relief and Works Agency (UNRWA) to assist the Palestinian refugees in the Middle East on a humanitarian basis, it also set up the UN High Commission for Refugees (UNHCR) to provide legal and other protection and promote the human rights of those refugees. But, again, for political reasons, this failed.[2]

It has been shown by different legal experts that no party has the right to negotiate away the inalienable rights of people. In this sense, not even the PLO has the right to sign a document foregoing the refugees' right to restitution and compensation. This issue remained a hurdle to peace as US diplomacy sidelined international law whenever it didn't suit its ends or Israel's position. Hence, former Secretary of State Madeleine Albright thought that these resolutions must be avoided because they were 'outdated' and could only create conflict. But will such an approach withstand the test of time and stability? Certainly not.[3]

Today, on the Israeli popular level, the refugee question is not the taboo it was around the negotiating table. A poll conducted by a group of Israeli and Palestinian researchers in Israel and the Occupied Territories found that 7 percent of Israeli Jews believe Israel holds the primary responsibility for the refugee problem, 5 percent believe it holds sole responsibility, and 35 percent recognize that responsibility to be both Jewish and Arab (almost the same percentage as among the Palestinians in the Occupied Territories, 41 percent). In other words, the majority of Israeli Jews admit partial or total responsibility for the refugee question. However, the majority of Israeli Jews, 90 percent, thought that the refugees should settle where they are today (57.2 percent) or in a future Palestinian state (32.2 percent). This certainly means that, although the road will be long and tortuous, it is nonetheless solid enough to allow the promotion of the political and legal rights of the refugees in Israel.

Compensation for the refugees has been estimated at between US$40-300 billion, depending on who makes the calculations and on what basis they are made. For example, a Palestinian economist, Atif Kubusi, has estimated that the compensation being demanded by the Jewish settlers of the Golan heights in return for their eventual evacuation could be the basis for calculations and, hence, a higher figure is more likely. During the Camp David negotiations, another figure leaked from consultants to the Palestinian delegation spoke of $40 billion in compensation, but that could not be confirmed. It was not clear if this referred to individual or national compensation, or both.

THE INTERNATIONAL COMMUNITY'S LASTING OBLIGATION

The international community's neglect of the question of the Palestinian refugees, as well as in the peace process, is inexcusable. There is no doubt that it is a tough issue that is both complicated and involves major risks for the parties, especially when we speak of two states – one Jewish and the other Palestinian. If the historical conditions are not suitable for a comprehensive solution, then at least certain Palestinians living in the dark camps of Lebanon and Gaza should have the right to return first, or else be compensated. Many might turn down the right to return to live among the Israeli Jews, and might prefer to be compensated in order to relocate. But what is of utmost importance in beginning to solve the refugee problem is for Israel to admit its historical responsibility for their predicament and begin to deal with the consequences of such responsibility along with, or in coordination with, the Palestinian state.

Israel also needs to come to terms with its own history. It must look in the mirror of the past and admit what, regrettably, it has long denied: moral and legal responsibility for, and hence, recognition in principle of the refugees' Right to Return or to compensation as stipulated in UN General Assembly Resolution 194. Only then will the vicious circle of conflict and violence begin to close, allowing for a new era of reconciliation and tolerance to ensue.

Moreover, after reaffirming for the hundredth time the Palestinians' Right of Return, the international community has a lasting obligation towards the refugees to ensure the implementation of their inalienable rights. This is a moral and legal responsibility.

NOTES

1. *Right of Return*, Badil, Bethlehem, May 2000, p. 15.
2. Susan Arram, 'Palestinian rights: failure under international law,' *Information Brief*, No. 40, Center for Policy Analysis on Palestine, Washington, DC, July 28, 2000.
3. Naseer Aruri, *Al-Hayat*, November 29, 2000.

6

JERUSALEM

KOLLEK We said things without meaning them, and we didn't carry them out. We said over and over that we would equalize the rights of Arabs and Jews in the city – empty talk ... Both Levi Eshkol and Menachem Begin promised them equal rights – both violated their promises ... Never have we given them a feeling of being equal before the law. They were and remain second- and third-class citizens.

JOURNALIST And this is said by a Mayor of Jerusalem who did so much for the city's Arabs, who built and paved roads and developed their neighborhoods?

KOLLEK Nonsense! Fairy tales! The Mayor developed nothing and built nothing! What did I do? Nothing. Sidewalks? Nothing! Cultural institutions? Not one. Yes, we installed a sewerage system for them and improved the water supply. Do you know why? Do you think it was for their good, for their welfare? Forget it! There were some cases of cholera there, and the Jews were afraid that they would catch it, so we installed sewerage and a water system.

TEDDY KOLLEK, FORMER MAYOR OF WEST JERUSALEM, TO *MAARIV*, OCTOBER 10, 1990, FOLLOWING THE TEMPLE MOUNT MASSACRE

THE OLD CITY: WHOSE CITY?

The Middle East peace process faltered at Camp David over the issue of the fate of Jerusalem. It proved to be the thorniest issue in the final status negotiations, although it could have been the easiest if it were not for the American and Israeli approaches, so outrageously in contradiction with UN Resolution 242, the basis of the peace process, and so infuriatingly insulting to the minds and sentiments of the Palestinian people. A few weeks after the failure of the summit, an Israeli assault on Jerusalem took the form of a provocative visit by Ariel Sharon to the Al-Aqsa Mosque. This triggered the bloody events at the Haram al-Sharif the next day, September 29, 2000, marking the beginning of the second Intifada. Another Israeli assault on Jerusalem had also been behind the clashes of 1996. It took the form of the Netanyahu government's decision to dig under the Moslem holy sites in Jerusalem for Jewish ruins.

The center of contention in Jerusalem is presumably the Old City and its immediate surroundings, which the Palestinians demand be handed back to them. Twenty-seven thousand Palestinians and only 2,000 Jews live in the Old City. In 1947, UN General Assembly Resolution 181 declared Jerusalem's status 'Corpus Seperatum.' This resolution was not implemented. After the 1948 war, which the Palestinians lost, a de facto division of the city ensued. The western part of Jerusalem, or 88 percent of the city, fell under Israeli control, and the eastern part, or twelve percent, under Jordanian control. Before that date, Muslim and Christian Palestinian estates comprised 54 percent of the city, while Jewish estates accounted for around 26 percent. The rest was municipal.[1]

On June 7, 1967, Israel occupied the eastern part of Jerusalem. On June 25, the Israeli government invented a legal cover for its annexation. At that time, Israel wanted to show the world that its aim was not to annex the city, but to provide the people with needed services. The careful wording used by Israel, 'jurisdiction' or 'administration,' would be extended to newly conquered areas. Needless to say, international law does not recognize unilateral annexation, even if it is carried out after a 'war of self-defense,' as Israel portrays its carefully prepared assault on its neighbors in 1967.

Since 1967, Israel has unilaterally expanded its boundaries of Jerusalem by annexing some 70 km. to the municipal boundaries of

West Jerusalem. Some 24 km. of that were expropriated primarily for the erection of new Jewish neighborhoods for which master plans were developed (so far covering 17.5 km.), while no such plans exist for the remaining 45 km. Only five sq. km. of the area for which master plans exist are allocated for Palestinian housing needs.[2]

In 1995, Israel uncovered its plans for the Greater Jerusalem metropolitan area exceeding 440 sq. km., three-quarters of which lies within the occupied pre-1967 borders and includes the ring settlements of Givat Ze'ev and Ma'ale Adumim. The Greater Jerusalem plan was meant, in part, to combat an expected demographic parity between Palestinians and Jews, largely due to the higher birth rate among the Palestinians. Israel expects the settler population to grow to 500,000 by 2015 when added to the population of West Jerusalem and the surrounding areas destined to be included in the 'umbrella municipality.' Arab Jerusalem will be physically separated from Ramallah and Bethlehem, encapsulated into Jewish Greater Jerusalem. The Barak government continued to implement the Greater Jerusalem plan which was supported by the late Yitzhak Rabin and even more vigorously by his successor Binyamin Netanyahu.[3] Ariel Sharon, who served as minister of infrastructure in Netanyahu's government and forcibly appropriated a Palestinian house for his own use in the Old City (the Arab quarter) of Jerusalem, has played a central role in advancing the settlement drive around Jerusalem in coordination with Mayor Ehud Olmert. When he became prime minister in 2001, the Judization of the city took a dramatic turn.

ISRAEL'S DEMOGRAPHIC WAR

The de facto annexation was executed by enacting two main laws. The first enabled Israel to extend its administration to the new occupied area, and the other law enabled the Israeli interior ministry to extend the city's municipal boundaries. This law applies to all municipalities, but in the case of Jerusalem it led to the enactment of two orders which extended the Jerusalem boundaries to cover 72 sq. km. Based on this decision, Israel was able to determine the number of people staying in this newly annexed area, and entitled them to ID cards which, since that time, have indicated residency rights rather than citizenship. According to the Palestinians, the decision was political, and reflected the Israeli desire to acquire as much land with as small an Arab population as possible. Since then Israel has encouraged Jewish residency in Metropolitan and East Jerusalem whose Jewish population has risen to over 190 thousand.

Israel's harsh measures against the Palestinians in East Jerusalem have continued in the last two years and showed no restraint during the last sixteen months of Barak's government. Barak exploited his good relations with the Clinton administration to evade implementing signed agreements. He expanded the settlements, and finished off what Netanyahu couldn't even begin – encircling Jerusalem through building construction in the Arab suburb of Abu Ghnaim, a project that had strained Arab-American and American-Israeli relations during Netanyahu's tenure.

And so continued the confiscation of ID cards from the Arab residents of Jerusalem – 2,200 between 1998 and 2001. In 1999, some 900 cases were received by Palestinian human rights organizations concerning 2,466 citizens. Nineteen citizens were deported. Thousands of citizens had their IDs withdrawn, only 78 got them back.[4] However, the policy of exclusion, or 'ethnic cleansing,' backfired. Instead of the number of Palestinians in the city being reduced, more Palestinians live in Jerusalem than ever before. Some 233,000 Palestinians, or three times the numbers in 1967, reside in East Jerusalem, according to the late Palestinian Minister for Jerusalem Faisal Husseini. Many of the city's residents who were living outside its boundaries have come back to Jerusalem in the last few years to escape Israeli ID confiscation.

At the beginning of 1999, the Israeli ministry of interior warned that more than twenty thousand houses had been built illegally in East Jerusalem. The Municipality of Jerusalem issued 141 demolition orders in 1999 and 19 were carried out. All in all, 92 homes have been demolished since the Oslo agreement was signed, leading to the displacement of hundreds of people in the city. Yet Israeli attempts to keep the demographic 'balance' of 73.5 versus 26.5 in favor of the Jews, has been torpedoed by Palestinian growth and allowed the shifting of the ratio to 33 percent versus 67 percent by the end of 1999.

Between 1967 and 1997, no more than 12 percent of all new buildings were built in Palestinian neighborhoods (most housing there was privately constructed), while the Israeli public sector constructed at least 40,000 housing units for Jews on expropriated land. In many ways, Israeli attempts to impose their version of the city as 'Jewish' in character have failed both demographically as well as spiritually. Exclusivism failed in Jerusalem, as the open multi-faith city won the day against Israeli policy.[5]

JERUSALEM IN THE FINAL STATUS NEGOTIATIONS

Realizing the sensitivity of the question of Jerusalem in the negotiations, the discussions centered, first and foremost, around sovereignty, but also touched on access, residency, and scope, or what constitutes the limits of the city. Israelis and Palestinians have agreed that Jerusalem should remain an open and undivided city; but they differed on the questions above mainly on sovereignty. Throughout the last seven years of negotiations, the two parties differed on the question of Jewish settlements established within the city boundaries, and on ending the current Israeli blockade of the city, which prevents the Palestinian population of the West Bank and Gaza from entering and denies them the right to residency in the city; another point of dispute was the Palestinian demand for the Right of Return for some 100,000 Arab Jerusalemites, forbidden from entering Jerusalem by the Israeli authorities. In other words, unilateral illegal actions by Israel in East Jerusalem have been the central problem facing the negotiations. According to the Fourth Geneva Convention, Israel had no right moving any part of its population to the newly conquered territories, and no right denying access to its Palestinian residents.

Before the Camp David negotiations started, Washington leaned towards a partial agreement that excluded Jerusalem from the 'framework agreement'. Only later did President Clinton feel that the resolution of the Jerusalem question was possible. However, the American delegation transmitted Israeli propositions that fell short of the minimum Palestinian aspirations on Jerusalem. Clinton's bridging proposals did not correspond to international legitimacy, nor specifically to UN Resolution 242, which called for withdrawal from the territories occupied in 1967.

During the Camp David II negotiations, Israel insisted that it impose its sovereignty over the Al-Aqsa Mosque and the Holy Sanctuary. All the clever formulas that were proposed by the American team were meant to mask this position. After the Palestinians rejected any such intrusion on their holy site, the Israelis and the Americans then demanded Israeli sovereignty over the land of the Mosque because, in their view, the Jewish Temple Mount was under the Moslem site, and hence Israel demanded that they have horizontal sovereignty over the site. They proposed in return that sovereignty over the Holy Sanctuary be transfered to an international body, constituted under the aegis of the UN Security Council and the Jerusalem Committee, that would give only trusteeship to the Palestinian state.

Moreover, Israel, via the United States, proposed different regimes for each neighborhood, a matter that would certainly have caused further atomization of the already divided city, instead of simply returning East Jerusalem to its lawful owners. Accordingly, what applied to the Christian neighborhood in the old city would not apply to the Armenian, and that would not apply to the Moslem neighborhood. Those three inner neighborhoods would have a different regime and separate legal standing from the neighborhoods in immediate proximity to the Old City such as Sheikh Jarrah, Sowana, Tour, Salah Eddin, Ras Al Amoud, and Silwan, for which the genies of Camp David proposed 'functional autonomy.' As for the outer neighborhoods such as Beit Hanina, Kufr Aqab, Kalandia, Sawahra, Samir Amis, Shufat and Esawiyyeh, which were not part of

Jerusalem until Israel occupied it and expanded its city limits, they would enjoy Palestinian sovereignty.

When these proposals were rejected, American delegates kept on switching neighborhood configurations until they proposed that both the outer and the inner neighborhoods would enjoy limited Palestinian sovereignty, but in the context of a different kind of Israeli security and legal arrangement guaranteeing the city's openness. However those arrangements remained unknown because Israel refused to give details until it received Palestinian approval of the principle regarding the old walled city. The Palestinians concluded that once the detailed arrangements were agreed, Israel would have insured effective Israeli control over the whole city.

It was also obvious that these solutions were even more problematic than the existing situation, and that they would create a far more divided city than exists today, hence allowing for more instability and Israeli intervention. There was nothing final about what the American and Israelis proposed at Camp David regarding Jerusalem; it all boiled down to maintaining Israeli de facto control of the overall area. At no point did any of the Israeli or American negotiators consider undoing the injustices done to Jerusalem, or at least address the harsh living conditions imposed on the Palestinians by the Israelis. In fact, Camp David came to cement those Israeli gains and legalize the illegal policy that Israel had implemented in East Jerusalem, including the illegal settlement on confiscated land, demolition of houses, confiscation of ID cards, and imposition of closures that choked the city economically and cut it off from its Palestinian hinterland.

After the failure of the summit, the Israeli government emphasized that all understandings reached at Camp David were null and void in the absence of an agreement. Alas, the Clinton administration consented to Israel's wishes instead of proposing that what had been achieved at Camp David become the grounds on which to continue the effort to reach a lasting solution for Jerusalem. The second Intifada forced Clinton to reiterate his positions in January before leaving office and Israeli Prime Minister

Ehud Barak moderated Israel's position at Taba, after Camp David, when he agreed to the principle of partitioning the city. He shattered the taboo of a 'united Jerusalem.'

SHARING THE CITY: END TO AN ISRAELI TABOO

Israel's position has moved closer to that of the international community, but it falls short of being a practical or just solution to the status of the embattled city. New Israeli voices have been speaking out in favor of division of the city and recognition of 'legitimate' Palestinian rights in it. A prominent political commentator in Israel's leading newspaper, *Haaretz*, wrote under the title 'The Courage to Divide': 'We will never see the end of the Palestinian-Israeli dispute and Jerusalem will become a scene of bloodshed for generations, unless we have the courage to say Yes, Jerusalem must be divided.'[6] Moreover, Meron Benvinisti, a historian and an ex-deputy mayor of Jerusalem, ridiculed what are termed 'creative' ideas on the city and insisted that only a division or sharing of Jerusalem could be viable in the long-term. Furthermore, the daily *Haaretz* has asked Barak to renounce the 'myth' that Israel could never surrender the Jewish holy places in the Dome of the Rock and the Holy Sanctuary, and emphasized that it was not in Israel's interest to have sovereignty over Moslem holy sites. This is certainly an important precedent that applies to the Christian places as well.

Before the outbreak of the confrontations, the Peace Now movement in Israel carried out a campaign under the slogan: One City, Capital of Two States. The campaign was so successful that the movement decided to expand on it. Israelis and six moderate members of the Israeli Jerusalem municipality also signed a petition that demanded the sharing of the city with the Palestinians as a capital of their state. Furthermore, polls showed an increasing number of Israelis accepting legitimate Palestinian rights to Jerusalem, including 55 percent of the governing Labor party supporters. On the official level, a no less important change had taken place. Traditionally, Israel has held a harsh position on the city, a stance that has increased of late. It insisted that it would not negotiate over its 'united capital' and if it were ever to do so, it would be only bilaterally with the Palestinians and without outside intervention. However, more recently, Israel moved to negotiate over the fate of the city and accepted, even encouraged, outside players to present their views and any 'creative' ideas they might have to resolve the issue. This is no longer on the table under Sharon.

THE POLITICS OF JERUSALEM TODAY

Today, the preoccupation in East Jerusalem is not so much about Israeli authority, or prospective Palestinian authority, but rather the lack of authority. Arab Jerusalemites continue to boycott elections to the Israeli city council, since they do not recognize it, and they receive less than 10 percent of the municipal budget despite making up 33 percent of the population. Nonetheless, a recent poll showed many preferring Israeli IDs in the city because of the liberty of movement and minimal rights they enjoy. But East Jerusalem is far from being integrated with West Jerusalem and Israelis hardly show up in the East.

Today there are 200 Palestinian institutions in East Jerusalem. However, Israel has continued to violate pledges it undertook towards the Palestinians of East Jerusalem in the last two years. It has often banned meetings of local NGOs and tried to close some, accusing them of being part of the PNA. The Orient House, a meeting place for NGOs, also continued to suffer from the isolation imposed by the Israelis, who refused to meet any international dignitaries who visited the PLO Negotiations Office there. Israel later occupied Orient House.

The Palestinians demand a political, not physical, separation in Jerusalem. Effectively, the Palestinians hope to see a divided sovereignty and shared control in the city. The Palestinians claim Al Quds (East Jerusalem), which comprises less than a quarter of the overall area of the Jerusalem of 1948 – the Israelis seized the other three-quarters of the city at that time, confiscated most of the Arab property there, and moved in all their government institutions, making Jerusalem their capital.

Yet despite the demographic changes in the city, there are no integrated neighborhoods in today's Jerusalem, and therefore neither sovereignty nor administrative authority should be a hurdle in the way of peace. Political separation between the Arab East and the Jewish West is now possible. This would take the form of symbolic shared or divided sovereignty rather than imposed barriers and blockades within the city boundaries, allowing for a fully open city.

As for the religious dimension affecting the city, there have been important developments that could ensure peaceful and open access to the holy places. A Vatican–PLO agreement signed on February 15, 2000, underlined the importance of 'freedom of religion,' 'freedom of conscience,' and the need to protect the equality of human and civil rights for all citizens in the Holy Land, particularly in the holy city. The document, which denounced the unilateral actions affecting Jerusalem, also insured that access to the Christian holy places be open and safeguarded. As for the Moslem and Jewish holy places, Arafat said recently that he recognizes that Jews who want to worship at the Buraq, or Western Wall, will enjoy security under full Israeli protection, a position echoed by Israel which asserted that a Moslem who wishes to worship in Al-Aqsa Mosque should not have to undergo Israeli security checks.

But there are no less important benefits for Israel once a just solution is found for Jerusalem. First, and presumably, most important for Israel, is security. As one of Israel's leading sociologists, Baruch Kimmerling, put it recently, sharing Jerusalem with the Palestinians as the capital of their state is the best way to safeguard the security of Israel in the long run. This view is ever more forthcoming in Israel. It is well known in the rather short Palestinian history of resistance that each time Israel has tried to block Palestinian resistance in one place, it has sprung up in another, as happened when the struggle moved from Palestine to Jordan, and later from Jordan to Lebanon, and later from Lebanon to the Intifada of the West Bank and Gaza after the Israeli invasion of Lebanon. If the parties do reach another agreement that will exclude Jerusalem, then violence and resistance will find their way into the city's streets, and those of the 'capital of Israel,' which no Israeli official or citizen looks forward to. For a number of reasons too complex to go into here, Israel has been relieved of any major Palestinian upheaval in Jerusalem. If that should take place, it will make Hebron and Gaza look like sideshows.

Second, international recognition: Israel's recognition of Palestinian rights to Al-Quds in East Jerusalem would pave the way for international recognition of its claim to Yerushalayim in West Jerusalem. So far, the international community considers Israel 'to be a military power in East Jerusalem and to have only a de facto authority over West Jerusalem.' In 1999, 149 countries to 1 voted in favor of a UN resolution that called Israel's decision to impose its laws and jurisdiction and administration in Jerusalem illegal and, therefore, null and void. All this could change.

Israel has much to gain in terms of the international recognition of its sovereignty over West Jerusalem, since sovereignty is embedded in the recognition of the international community. It has nothing to lose from handing over the *de facto* occupied Al-Quds, and much to gain in terms of sovereignty over the Jewish Quarter and the Wailing Wall of the Old City if the Egyptian initiative is adopted. Today, not one of the 192 sovereign states recognizes Israel's sovereignty over Jerusalem. Tomorrow all or most of them will. Sovereignty for Palestinians in their part, sovereignty for Israel in its part, and an open city with joint municipal administration and control. Otherwise, what a waste of time and human energy… and life.

Today there are rational ways to satisfy conflicting claims in the city. If the parties intend to reach a final settlement, then the issue of Jerusalem must be resolved. The city should be seen as an asset rather than a hurdle in the negotiations. In a sense, Jerusalem should be the engine for peace; a force of stability and coexistence rather than a by-product of the peace process or, worse, a source of division and conflict.

Israel's exclusivism and narrow claim to the city has been dropped as the idea of sharing the city emerged, albeit timidly, as the pragmatic and probable solution for Jerusalem. International pressure on Israel (and on the United States) yielded many benefits as Washington pushed Prime Minister Barak to accept certain compromises in the city. The 'Clinton Paper' presented to the Palestinians in early January reflects this change. It is certain that the international position on Jerusalem is winning the day, slowly but consistently. In the words of one scholar, people are realizing that Jerusalem, like any other city, has water and sewage running according to the laws of gravity, and therefore needs a resolution that deals with its living people and not only its past dynasties, because Jerusalem belongs first and foremost to its citizens. And yet, Jerusalem is also a very special city with a unique character, which in effect means that it must accommodate various beliefs and traditions.

NOTES

1. Khalil Tofkajy, *The Settlements in Jerusalem: Goals and Results*, 1999, www.Palestinegd.fi_oriant.html
2. Ir Shalem, *East Jerusalem – The Current Planning Situation. A Survey of Municipal Plans and Planning Policy*, 1998.
3. LAW, *Report on Jerusalem*, 1998.
4. LAW, *Plans for a 'Greater Jerusalem,'* June 5, 2000.
5. B'tselem Report, 1999; Ir Shalem, *East Jerusalem – The Current Planning Situation. A Survey of Municipal Plans and Planning Policy*, 1998.
6. *Haaretz*, August 30, 2000.

APARTHEID

7

SEVEN FAT YEARS FOR ISRAEL – SEVEN LEAN YEARS FOR PALESTINE

Since the signing of the Oslo Agreement, the economic situation has continued to deteriorate [in the West Bank and Gaza]. The decline in household incomes, a sharp increase in unemployment, and the general broadening of poverty pose serious challenges for economic sustainability.

WORLD BANK REPORT, 1997

The peace process has been an economic necessity for Israel, the US and the Palestinians. For America, the leader of the global era, the Arab-Israeli conflict is no longer the asset it was during the Cold War, rather a hindrance to the post-Gulf war Pax-Americana in the Middle East. The Arab-Israeli conflict was seen by the Clinton administration as a barrier to a sweeping era of globalization that was banging on the gates of the Middle East.

In the nineties, for Israel, the most powerful country in the region, a decade of economic liberalization and privatization, and the recent immigration of a million ex-Soviet Jews, necessitated an economic breakthrough. An ambitious and ever more influential business community in Israel believed two ingredients were necessary for such a breakthrough. The first was a US-supported entry into the emerging global market that would attract foreign investments. Second, in order to 'globalize,' Israel had to restructure its colonial economic ties to the West Bank and Gaza, particularly after six years of the Intifada (1987–1993) had disrupted the stability of the West Bank and Gaza Strip and severed their relationship with Israel.

As for the Palestinians in the 1990s, any economic change in their desperate situation after the Gulf war was progress. The Occupied Territories were suffering from the recession and economic depression caused by the long years of the Intifada. Moreover, financial revenues from the Gulf states had diminished to almost zero after the Gulf war. This was the case not only for the PLO, which went bankrupt, but also for the people. Money transfers from Palestinian expatriates in the Gulf diminished, while more than 300,000 Palestinians were driven out of Kuwait. As a result, an end to the conflict was urgent for the Palestinians in order to put an end to unemployment, poverty, and the personal and national humiliation that had only worsened after three decades of occupation.

However, as they realized later, their economic conditions could deteriorate even further 'thanks' to the Oslo process. After seven years of the 'peace process,' the Palestinians are worse off today than they were in 1993 while, alas, Israel has continued to prosper beyond the wildest expectations.

OSLO AS AN ECONOMIC DOCUMENT

The Oslo Declaration of Principles (DOP) was accurately described as 'primarily an economic document,' because, among other things, 'two-thirds of it is devoted to describing the functions of eight PLO-Israeli committees whose job it is to harness ... a degree of mutual economic interest that exceeds any agreement signed between the two states.' No wonder the Economic Protocols between the two parties were signed before the 'Gaza and Jericho first' agreement was signed in May 1994 (giving limited autonomy to 65 percent of the Gaza Strip and Jericho).[1]

Prior to Oslo, the Western approach to the so-called 'economics of peace' was narrated in studies and assessments in cooperation with Israeli economists, officials, and business representatives. As usual, the Palestinians were unprepared, and so were the Arabs, who had improvised ever since the bilateral economic relations – the central component of the peace accords – came to bear on the negotiations. The economic component of Oslo continued to haunt the economically backward Arabs and Palestinians in the form of long-term arrangements, contracts, cooperation commitments, and investment, all of which they were far from ready to deal with. Within seven years, four major world economic summits on the Middle East took place, in Casablanca, Amman, Cairo and Doha to underline the centrality of economics to the peace process. The party with the most to gain from these summits was Israel. It also benefited from the World Economic Forum's approach to the Middle East during its annual meetings.

Tel Aviv University, the Israel Chamber of Commerce, the World Bank, Harvard's Kennedy School of Government, the Council on Foreign Relations, the Brookings Institution, and others all concerned themselves with the peace economy. Meanwhile, Israel's high-tech industries continued to attract top multinationals such as Intel, IBM, Motorola, Vishay, Tower Semiconductors, and others.

Thanks to international investment in Israel's high-tech industry after the beginning of the peace process, Israel's economic stature grew beyond imagination. Israel was soon in a position to employ its highly skilled and educated Russian immigrants who, instead of being a burden on the state in this sensitive period, turned out to be an important economic asset. In 1995–1999 Israel's GDP rose by almost 50 percent – or from 264 to 410 billion shekels – while its population rose by only 10 percent in the same period.[2]

According to the Israeli Chamber of Commerce, during the previous four decades Israel had lost some US$40 billion in potential exports because of the Arab boycott.[3] Since that was lifted, all has changed. More than twenty countries established diplomatic relations with Israel in 1994, and more have followed since. The lifting of those measures opened up new markets in southern Asia and South America, as well as in the Middle East and other regions. In 1994, Israeli exports to Asia increased by over a third, and exports to India rose by more than a half, while exports to Thailand rose by about 70 percent. By 1995, China, one of the most important markets for Israeli civilian and military industries, that had long boycotted Israel because of the Arab-Israeli conflict, had opened its doors to Israel. Overall exports to Asia rose by 25 percent.[4]

Israel added a new twist to the term 'peace dividend' when it profited from military investments instead of gaining from savings in the defense sector. Research and development that was subsidized by the US, but was still a drain on the economy, has become a flourishing field since Oslo. By the mid-1990s, Israel had signed cooperation agreements in science, technology, research and development, civil aviation, and intelligence gathering with Russia, Turkey, Singapore, India, France, Ukraine, and South Africa. Its relations with the latter were especially interesting as Apartheid was being abolished there while it was being established in Palestine. Significant defense contracts were being signed with the reborn state.[5]

Meanwhile, the business sector share of the GDP grew by 39 percent between 1990 and 1994. Israel's rise in imports, mostly investment goods, and high subsidies to foreign companies who made a base for themselves in Israel, have been seen as a positive economic indicator, as they enhance long-term investment that could only strengthen the Israeli economy. Per capita income rose from $12,600 in 1992 to $15,600 in 1995, and is expected to top $20,000 by the end of 2001. Just as importantly, and despite the huge immigration from the ex-Soviet Union, unemployment in Israel was reduced from 11.2 percent in 1992 to 6.9 percent in 1995, another very positive indicator, especially when taking into consideration that Israel imported over 300,000 foreign workers from Romania, Thailand, and other places.[6]

Much of this process created a new class of upwardly mobile Israeli professionals and businessmen, who became internationalist in their target markets and globalist in their outlook and who cared less about continuing the seizure of the Occupied Territories. This powerful Israeli nouveau riche, who frequently rubbed shoulders with their Western counterparts, became convinced that the time had come to rid Israel of the negative image of occupier as being bad for business. This opened the door to two different outlooks. One totally reliant on relations with the West, preferring to look westward to Europe and the US, putting less emphasis on the East, the Occupied Territories, and the Arab world. The other view, especially prevalent among those in small industries who relied on cheap Palestinian labor and on the Palestinian market for their products, agreed that it was perhaps time to transform economic relations with the Palestinians in a way that guaranteed long-term stability, but insisted on the need to insure continued Israeli domination. Once the peace process brought with it the promise of stability, the second view won the day in the Occupied Territories; rather than evacuate the territories, Israel restructured its relations with the inhabitants on a patron–client basis.

THE IMPACT OF OSLO ON THE PALESTINIAN ECONOMY

The peace process failed to deliver to the Palestinians the minimum economic benefits – considered necessary by the US and like-minded-people – in order for them to swallow the bitter political compromises of Oslo and accept the dependency relationship with Israel. The silver spoon was needed particularly when Israel violated the accords. But economic progress for the Palestinians was anything but forthcoming, as the light at the end of the tunnel finally went out after years of their economic, social, and cultural rights being violated. When asked how they viewed their economic conditions since the beginning of the Oslo process, the Palestinians called a spade a spade, not a spoon. Fifty percent of Gazan respondents to a poll in 2000 said their standard of living had worsened, and 42.9 percent of West Bankers shared the same view. Indeed, the standard of living and quality of life had dwindled since Oslo began and the Palestine National Authority was established.[7]

Throughout the process, the Palestinians suffered higher poverty rates, greater unemployment, and less access to education and health care than before the negotiations began. According to World Bank officials, usually conservative in their estimates: 'The central story of the West Bank and Gaza Strip economy in the past few years is one of deterioration even though positive developments have also occurred since 1993 with the transfer of some areas of authority to the Palestinian Authority.' Although new roads were paved, new classrooms opened, and sewerage networks inaugurated in a number of places, thanks to US$3 billion in international aid (the highest in the world after Israel and Bosnia), nonetheless, six years after it began, Oslo led to a 20 percent decrease in per capita incomes. Hardly the basis on which to build support for the process.

In 1997, World Bank experts warned that 'Since the signing of the Oslo Agreement, the economic situation has continued to deteriorate. The decline in household incomes, a sharp increase in unemployment, and the general broadening of poverty pose serious challenges for economic sustainability.' Given the loss of jobs abroad, the most pressing challenges were to remove some of the constraints facing domestic production. However, the situation only deteriorated further as the contraints persisted. The little good news that international organizations prided themselves with in the last two years of the peace process, such as a surge in employment, or a few points rise in GDP, have been too little too late. In fact, they were not characteristic of what might lie ahead. Needless to say, the fact that tens of thousands of Palestinians slip into Israel illegally should not be considered a sign of a properous economy.

The Palestinian economy is very small, the GDP is US$3.6 billion in comparison to Israel's almost $100 billion. Palestinian exports are also low – $750 million compared to Israel's $25 billion – and its imports, which exceed $3.4 billion, are a tenth of Israel's imports. The income from work abroad is about $900 million, and income from tax agreements with Israel reaches about $600 million. All of these components of the Palestinians' economy have been totally dependent on Israel.[8] In fact, more than 88 percent of Palestinian exports go to Israel, while the Palestinian territories are the second destination of Israeli exports after America, reaching $2.5 billion.

Israel's control methods have deepened the disparities between Israel and the Palestinians. According to the World Bank Brief in August 2000, Israeli-imposed closures, for political reasons or security justifications, have led to 'movement restrictions which impact the ability of Palestinian workers to access jobs in Israel and of Palestinian goods to access the Israeli market and Israeli ports of entry and exit.' Hence Israeli one-way closures during the first three and a half years caused the Palestinians a loss of one billion dollars and a drop of 36 percent in the per capita Gross National Product, according to a UN report published on April 3, 1997.[9]

SEPARATION BECOMES SEGREGATION

Palestinian labor was by and large excluded from the Israeli market place after Oslo and the policy of 'separation' translated into segregation and closures. The unemployment sky-rocketed as a result of saturation in the weakened industrial and agricultural sectors caused by closures, expensive transportation and security barriers. To make things worse, Israel began to issue permits to those allowed to work in Israel, leading to a dramatic decline of Palestinian employment in Israel from 116 thousand in 1992 to 28,500 in 1996. The rate of unemployment in Palestine was 18.2 percent in September 1995, only to climb to 28.4 percent in 1996. According to World Bank estimates, this was higher than all 57 countries surveyed. Roughly 20 to 25 percent are unemployed during 'normal times,' and the figure goes up to 30 percent, and even to above 40 percent during closures such as in the recent Intifada period. Overall, a mere one-half to two-thirds employment capacity of the Palestinians has been satisfied in recent years.

Naturally, unemployment translated into rising poverty and misery in the Occupied Territories. According to World Bank figures, poverty continued to rise, especially during severe unemployment periods, reaching, in 1997, 40 percent of Gazans and almost 20 percent of the West Bank, with the highest being in the refugee camps (50 percent) and in rural areas. In many cases where Palestinians did reach work in Israel illegally, their salaries dropped dramatically. Israel's method of reducing the number of Israeli permits to workers, while knowing that as many as tens of thousands could still cross the Green Line anyway, renders hundreds of thousands of family members under constant fear for their parents or siblings, who could be arrested by the Israelis, or who could not cross because the closures might be too tight for them to reach the 'land of milk and honey'.[10]

In this sense, Barak's threats of 'economic separation' in the spirit of Rabin's slogan, 'Getting Gaza out of Tel Aviv,' meant indiscriminate mass punishment of a whole people under occupation by strangling their economy. So did the hermetic closures of the Autonomous Territories for political maneuvers, or after each violent incident initiated by Jews or Palestinians, which translated into holding the entire Palestinian population hostage to cynical Israeli calculations.

According to an editorial of Israel's leading paper *Haaretz*:

Encirclement, or more bluntly, siege, of Palestinian villages lacks even a pretence of having a security purpose – this is a real tool of severe and collective punishment. Encirclement of villages completely disrupts the day-to-day lives of the Palestinian people. Residents find it difficult, or are totally unable, to move from one area to another for work, trade, or education, and they cannot get basic services. Encirclement has partially put many educational institutions in the territories out of action, has completely stopped production in factories and work in offices. It is not rare to witness some real suffering that encirclement causes residents, such as sick patients who fail to get to hospitals for medical treatment.[11]

ISRAEL RESTRUCTURES ECONOMIC RELATIONS WITH PALESTINIANS

The economic model adopted for the Occupied Territories during the peace process was financed by the World Bank and the international community, but was thought out by special working groups in Israeli and American institutions. Numerous studies tackled different aspects of present and future Israeli economic relations with the Palestinians and the Arabs. Israeli economist Ezra Sadan wrote the blueprints that became the basis for restructuring Palestinian economic dependency vis-à-vis Israel. The Oslo process came to implement the slogan 'Get Gaza out of Tel Aviv' by bringing Tel Aviv businesses to Gaza. Israeli industrial needs and demands were satisfied in Gaza and the West Bank through large, official, and clandestine subcontracting relations that exploited cheap Palestinian labor without having Palestinians inside the Green Line.

Israel's blueprints foresaw a Palestinian economy fully dependent and, hence, independent Palestinian domains were 'encouraged to disintegrate.' According to Sadan's 'industrial parks' concept, or Mequilladoras, Israel was to improve on the subcontracting formula by developing certain industrial areas in the midst of seas of poverty and backwardness that would allow cheap labor to be more productive and more responsive to Israeli industrial demands. This was an updated version of the same model developed in South Africa called 'growth points.'

But in order for the plan to work in the long-term, a 'competent' or legitimate 'Palestinian Authority' was needed to supervise a smooth transition to the new dependency relationship and in order to avoid any more Intifadas that would disrupt the economic environment. Enter the PLO, an organization suddenly committed to, and enthusiastic about, free-market principles and open borders between Israel and the Palestinians. Interestingly enough, most of the Palestinians who expressed their disappointment with their economic conditions in the following years did so by negatively associating the advent of Oslo with the appearance of the PNA and blaming it on both, while at the same time, as the polls show, they continued to have a positive political view of the leadership of Yasser Arafat.[12]

A number of Palestinian officials, 'consultants,' and 'advisors' went into high gear with the Israeli planning. They constituted a new class of profiteers, VIPs, who depended heavily on the continuation of the peace process, regardless of its fairness or adequacy. These VIPs benefited from the 'economics of peace' and from the 'peace industry' that was dominated by Israelis under the auspices of the World Bank and the European Community and were allowed to travel relatively freely. A new network of security chiefs, officials, and their kin, along with businessmen, had a stake in the process. They participated in the joint ventures with Israelis, traded with Israeli goods, subcontracted cheap labor, and had exclusive contracts with international financial organizations. Very few got involved in a productive or independent Palestinian economy and the majority took on the role of middlemen between Israeli industries and cheap Palestinian labor and consumers.

This network was strengthened by American and European support of 'cooperation' projects between Palestinians and Israelis that paid lip service to genuine Palestinian needs for minimum independence. The likes of the American 'Builders for Peace,' headed by then Vice President Al Gore, and the European Commission for Mediterranean Affairs supported primarily joint-venture type projects. Such approaches deepened the dependency of Palestinians on Israelis instead of nurturing a Palestinian economy. The Palestinian and Israeli middlemen who exploited the notion of 'joint ventures' looked for short-term profits and ignored the consequences of the long-term dependency relationship they were nourishing with Israel.

In the absence of any system of taxation, representation, and transparency, corruption inevitably grew among those who benefited from this master–servant relationship. Corrupt VIPs became clients who had to answer to their patrons, but also had to be responsive to the demands of their Palestinian victims in order to remain effective. When economic conditions worsened in Palestine, Israel's blackmail of the clients intensified. Corruption was the inevitable result of Oslo.

In the process, the share of public expenditures to GDP increased from 12 percent in 1994 to more than 25 percent in 1999, mostly to employ over 100,000 people (one-fourth of total domestic employment), a substantial number among them for police forces. The Authority kept on augmenting its employees to absorb unemployment and to insure a 'peaceful' transition. As a result, foreign aid allowed more employment and substituted for lack of taxation, hence turning the phrase 'taxation translates into representation' on its head, as accountability to the people was substituted by accountability to the donors' gatekeeper, America. In other words, the PNA was more accountable to Washington, Israel, and the World Bank than to its own citizens.[13]

BEING AN ECONOMIC DEPENDENCY

The Oslo process has been used as an instrument by Israel to insure its economic power over the Palestinians. Israel hoped to achieve through the American-sponsored peace process what it couldn't achieve by war – notably regional domination, the sort of domination that abandons the rule of force and the capability of inflicting physical harm from outside the society, in favor of the capacity to shape and influence national and socio-economic priorities from deep down inside. Nonetheless, partly because of wishful thinking and partly overplaying its hand, Israel could not go all the way to materialize its economic hegemony. Its international success was not matched in the Occupied Territories where Israeli hegemony remained one of physical force, especially in light of pressure from the Israeli army. However, Israel has done the Palestinian economy so much harm that it is hard to envision any future relationship in the short and intermediate terms that would not involve dependency.

With the outbreak of the Intifada, Israeli economic relations with the outside world suffered, but continued to show signs of growth, regardless of the deterioration on the ground and the damage to a few badly hit sectors, such as tourism. Interestingly, several Israeli companies that trade on the New York Stock Exchange were also hit soon after the second Intifada broke out.

The Barak government continued to assure Israel's business community two months into the Intifada that the country was doing well overall. And the Central Bank head expected no more than a 1 or 2 percent drop in growth in 2000. But the Tel Aviv business community, which has a better feel for the effects of the Intifada on the economy, continued to be anxious.

For the Palestinians, however, Israel's refusal to evacuate or redeploy from the majority of the Occupied Territories, withdrawing only from pockets of human misery that continued to be encircled by military units and settlements, further contributed to the worsening of the economic arrangements. This trend was changing the priorities of the peace process from insuring the viability, or the livability, of a Palestinian entity to insuring the viability of the Palestine National Authority as the guardian of the precarious stability. While the standard of living continued to fall to less than 60 percent of its pre-Oslo level, according to the Clinton administration's own figures, security expenditures remained very high. One-third of the meagre Palestinian budget went to security expenditures at the insistence of the US and Israel to maintain stability during the continuous impasse.[14]

In fact, the security budget of the PNA grew so high that, by 1999, it was bigger than the health, social services, and education budgets combined. The PNA was obliged to use undemocratic and illegal measures against its population in order to be considered an 'acceptable partner' and eligible for American aid. As a consequence, the PNA employed sixteen policemen for every thousand inhabitants, or four times the number in Israel. This imbalance in priorities led to a political crisis. Several Palestinian legislative members, opposition leaders, and other independent popular leaders signed a document at the end of November 1999 accusing the PNA of corruption and misuse of the national budget for non-productive security expenditures. But Washington and Israel showed total disregard for the plight of the people as they pushed for even higher security spending.

The sad fact that the PNA went along with Israeli plans, instead of offering the Palestinians an overall independent long-term development policy for the entire Palestinian territories, meant that the Palestinians would be destined to become ever more dependent on the goodwill of Israel, and, in the process, weaker, more underdeveloped, and corrupt. Moreover, Israel encouraged and exploited Palestinian private initiatives, mostly in subcontracting that amounted to slave labor. Palestinian women in the textile sweatshops of Gaza and the West Bank earned US$3 a day.

At the outbreak of the second Intifada, Israel launched an all-out economic war against the people and the PNA. It withheld hundreds of million of dollars it had collected from Palestinians in taxes, although it was legally obliged to hand all the money over to the PNA. Moreover, in the first six weeks of the Intifada, the Palestinian economy lost all that it had received from the donor countries throughout the year. At least US$10-15 million was being lost daily, according to Palestinian and World Bank estimates. Less than six months after the outbreak of the Intifada, a United Nations report of March 2001 considered the consequences of closing the Occupied Territories as the worst since 1967, and warned against the deteriorating standard of living that produced a new record of one million Palestinians living under the poverty line, up from 645 thousand just a few months earlier. It also predicted an increase in poverty reaching 43.8 percent of all Palestinians in the West Bank and Gaza by the end of 2001, regardless of whether the closures are eased. The number of handicapped and injured rose beyond 10,000, in itself a major future burden on the Palestinian economy. Israel has in effect conducted an all-out war on the Palestinian economy and infrastructure in order to weaken Palestinian resolve, cripple the PNA, and discredit the Palestinians in the international community as a non-viable and unworthy peace and economic partner.

With such an economic partner, who needs enemies? It's hard to ignore the deliberate policy of stifling the Palestinian economy and erecting security, geographical, political, and economic barriers in the way of its natural or independent growth, in order to make it yet more dependent on Israel's economy and strategy. When the dust settles after the second Intifada, and regardless of who backs out first or what new arrangement is reached, Israel will come out economically dominant, and the Palestinians will be in need of help and, probably in the short term, of the dependency relations that have led to their misery. Under such circumstances, insuring the flow of cheap labor to Israel has unfortunately become a Palestinian national priority.

Without just peace, there will be more dependency and less Palestinian prosperity. Certainly, healthy economic relations could lend a hand to peaceful efforts while business dealings could enhance stability, but in the absence of an equitable political solution, economic relations become a tool of oppression and subjugation, as has been the case with Israeli hegemony in Palestine over the last seven lean years. Increasingly, as socio-economic dependency deepens in the minuscule territories of Israel-Palestine, the appalling economic conditions will become an Israeli socio-political dilemma as much as they are a Palestinian national challenge.

NOTES

1. Graham Usher, *Middle East International*, London, January 21, 1994.
2. Emma C. Murphy, 'The Arab-Israeli peace process: responding to the economic globalization,' *Critique*, Fall 1996, pp. 80–81; Country Report, *Economist Intelligence Unit*, August 2000, UK, p. 6.
3. Allan Ritzky, 'Peace in the Middle East: what does it really mean for Israeli business,' *Columbia Journal of World Business*, Vol. 30, No. 3, Fall 1995, p. 28.
4. Emma C. Murphy, 'The Arab-Israeli peace process: responding to the economic globalization,' *Critique*, Fall 1996, p. 77.
5. *Defense News*, July, 25–31, 1994.
6. Emma C. Murphy, 'The Arab-Israeli peace process: responding to the economic globalization,' *Critique*, Fall 1996, p. 77.
7. Birzeit University survey: 'Priorities under a Palestinian State,' 2000.
8. *World Bank Report 2000*.

9. Cited in *Oslo's Final Status and Future of the Middle East*, CPAP, Washington, 1997, p. 1.

10. *World Bank Report on the West Bank and Gaza, 2000*.

11. *Haaretz*, January 8, 2001.

12. Birzeit University survey: 'Priorities under a Palestinian State,' 2000.

13. 'West Bank and Gaza in Brief,' World Bank, August, 2000.

14. Assistant Secretary Martin Indyk, 'Testimony on the Mideast Peace Process to the Senate Appropriations Committee,' distributed by the United States Information Agency.

8

THE WEST BANK SETTLEMENTS: APARTHEID IN PRACTICE

It is symbolic that no country in the world (except South Africa) recognizes Ciskei, just as there is no country in the world that recognizes the Jewish settlements in Judea and Samaria.

YOUSF SCHNEIDER, CISKEI'S ISRAEL REPRESENTATIVE, DURING CEREMONIES HELD IN THE ISRAELI-OCCUPIED WEST BANK SETTLEMENT OF ARIEL, TWINNING IT WITH CISKEI'S 'CAPITAL', BISHO

If the Palestinians were black, Israel would be now a pariah state subject to economic sanctions led by the United States. Its development and settlement of the West Bank would be seen as a system of Apartheid, in which the indigenous population was allowed to live in a tiny fraction of its own country, in self-administered 'bantustans' with 'whites' monopolizing the supply of water and electricity. And just as the black population was allowed into South Africa's white areas in disgracefully under-resourced townships, so Israel's treatment of Israeli Arabs – flagrantly discriminating against them in housing and education spending – would be recognized as scandalous, too ...

EDITORIAL, *THE OBSERVER*, LONDON, OCTOBER 15, 2000

Ever since the beginning of the peace process in 1993, an unrelenting Israeli settlement drive in the Occupied Territories has undermined the possibility of reaching a just solution to the Palestinian-Israeli conflict. In fact, it has aggravated the situation and contributed in a major way to the outbreak of the second Intifada. The settlement drive persevered in complete contradiction to UN resolutions, and in direct violation of the 1949 Fourth Geneva Convention Relative to the Protection of Civilian Persons in Time of War, which was signed by Israel and the US. The convention forbids the transfer of any segment of the population of an occupying force to its occupied territories. The settlement policy is also in violation of the principles of the Oslo process, which specified in article 31 that 'neither side shall initiate or take any step that will change the status of the West Bank and the Gaza Strip pending the outcome of the permanent status negotiations.' The settlement expansion has continued unabated and undisturbed since the seventies, and accelerated after the launch of the peace process. The international community, and the official US position, has considered the settlements illegal and 'destructive' to reaching a permanent peace. In numerous statements by the UN, the US, and the European Union, Israeli colonization was considered a land-mine in the way of peaceful settlements.

Not only are the settlements a hurdle in the negotiations, they constitute an accelerating and aggravating factor that ignites confrontations and instigates violence in the Occupied Territories. More importantly, they are a destabilizing and complicating factor in any post-peace settlement. Israel's strategy of maintaining its settlements intact is meant to ensure maximum Israeli territorial expansion and economic domination within the territories occupied after 1967. Israeli control over water resources and the electricity supply, in addition to its increasing economic activity and investment in the settlements and industrial zones close to them, has led to a quasi-Apartheid system encompassing three or four Palestinian 'bantustans' segregated by Israeli settlements and security posts. The American-Israeli proposal to end the conflict envisions Palestine's indigenous population living in self-administered, fractured, discontinuous, underdeveloped, and under-resourced territories, surrounded by economically superior Israelis with overriding security authority.

Meanwhile, the Jewish settlers in the Occupied Territories have emerged as the most violent element in those areas and have dictated Israel's policy there since the late 1970s. They established their own paramilitary and terrorist organizations, at times supported by the Israeli army. They have been active in lynching Palestinians and attacking their property. In the 1980s the terrorist settler network was responsible for the attacks on elected Palestinian mayors in the West Bank. A few months after the peace process began, one Baruch Goldstein, a settler from the Hebron area, massacred some twenty-nine Palestinians during their prayers in the Ibrahimi Mosque in Hebron. In the second Intifada, the settlers were responsible for a large, but unspecified, number of Palestinian killings in the Occupied Territories, including a number of victims who were lynched and killed.

The settlers' illegal presence paved the way for a dual system of control, an Apartheid system, which has taken root in the West Bank and Gaza Strip. The main thrust of Palestinian suffering and desperation has resulted from this system — created by the Labor governments, supported by Likud, and executed by the Israeli military under the cover of the Oslo process and with the direct financial and political support of the donor countries, notably Europe and the US. Israel used the cover of the Oslo process to repackage its colonialism by setting up major blocs of settlements connected with a network of roads and by-pass roads that were especially carved through the besieged territories for the sake of maintaining normal life in the settlements. Paradoxically, Israel erected its Apartheid system at the same time that the world got rid of Apartheid in South Africa.

EXPANSION OF THE SETTLEMENTS

When the peace process started in Madrid there were about 75,000 settlers in the West Bank and Gaza. The figure went up to 95 thousand prior to the signing of the Oslo agreement and climbed by 50 percent – from 95,000 to 147,000 settlers – between 1993 and 1996, when Israel was governed by the Labor party. Under Prime Minister Binyamin Netanyahu, settlement growth continued at a frantic pace and accelerated further during the eighteen months of Barak's government. Housing development in the settlements in 2000 was pursued at twice the pace of the previous year, as Israeli bulldozers continued their work on a large network of security roads linking settlements and creating barriers to the return of more land to the Palestinians. Today there are over 190,000 settlers in the West Bank, 5,000-7,000 in Gaza, 17,000 in the Golan, and 190,000 in East Jerusalem.

During the last seven years and more, the annual growth of settler populations in the West Bank and Gaza was three to four times the annual population growth in Israel. In 1999 the growth was a high 14 percent. The same applies to Israeli building work in the Occupied Territories, where areas and dwellings under construction witnessed an important increase after Oslo was signed, and most evidently since Barak marched into office. According to Peace Now statistics, the Barak government issued tenders for the construction of some 3,196 housing units in some sixteen settlements between July and December of 1999.[1] At the beginning of the year 2000, settlers challenged Barak by erecting forty-two new illegal outposts, and Barak assented to the settlers by allowing thirty of them to remain intact. In a new five-year settlement expansion plan, Barak's ministry of housing began to build, among others, 12,000 new dwellings in West Bank settlements – in the areas of Kiryat Arba, the settlement adjacent to Hebron, and Ariel in the middle of the West Bank, and a further 3,000 in Ma'ale Adumim, east of Jerusalem – with a governmental subsidy of US$17,000 for each buyer.[2]

After the signing of the May 1994 Cairo Agreement, Israel began to enhance its links with the settlements in the affected areas through the construction of a network of roads that bypass Palestinian areas. Barak, like his predecessors, opposed placing any territorial constraints on the settlements' well-being. The signing of the Oslo agreement envisioned Israel's redeployment in almost 85 percent of the West Bank. Instead, the application of the accords confined the Palestinians to 227 non-contiguous islands. These islands constitute 40 percent of the West Bank, only one-quarter of which are under full Palestinian civil and security control, or so-called area A. Traditionally, the Labor Party has been more discreet than Likud.

Today, Israel still retains a bloc of four settlements at Ma'ale Adumim, an area larger than Tel Aviv, in order to consolidate its control over 'highways, hilltops, and crossroads,' effectively paralysing transportation throughout the country. So essential to its 'matrix of control' are Israel's settlements, that the residents 'don't think of themselves as settlers anymore.' According to the American Middle East expert, Don Peretz, 'If established under today's circumstances, the Palestinian "state" will be a crippled, barely continuous land mass penetrated by Israeli settlements on all sides, with most towns and villages surrounded by Israeli roads and security forces. This tiny, misshapen space will have little internal integrity, and no room for expansion of its fast-growing populace, or for diaspora Palestinians who want to return. Cut off from Jordan and almost entirely dependent on Israel for such vital necessities as water and electricity, the state's economic potential will be severely limited.'

When the Camp David summit began, Israel had almost 200,000 settlers in 200 settlements in the Occupied Territories, and direct jurisdiction over five percent of the West Bank. However, it was not so much the size of the area they occupied that was important, as the way they cut through the West Bank from North to South and from East to West with by-pass roads, disrupting any geographical continuity for the Palestinians. This ever-growing settler community within the Israeli-controlled area, accounting for 59 percent of the West Bank and 20 percent of Gaza, has allowed the introduction of new infrastructure and institutions, all of which enjoy extra-legal and extra-territorial status and are 'all but indistinguishable from Israel proper.' Since the Oslo process began, Israel has confiscated 273,000 hectares for settlement expansion, 150,000 during Rabin's and 23,000 during Barak's mandate.[3]

Like his predecessors, Barak considered the settlements integral parts of the Zionist idea. He believed Israel has the right to settle in the occupied Palestinian territories. He stated that there is no meaning to the Israeli identity 'without the connection to Shilo and to Tekoa, to Bet El and to Efrat.' In a way, Barak saw any emerging Palestinian state as confining itself and circumscribing its sovereignty to Israeli security and settlement demands just as Netanyahu called for reducing and delineating the powers of the Palestinian entity and its territoriality.

In fact, as arbitration over the final status negotiations was underway at Camp David, Barak treated the territories, where some 80 percent of the settlers live, as if they were already annexed to Israel. Paradoxically, the Camp David summit clarified the ambiguity that overshadowed the Israeli and American positions on the settlements. Barak underlined the fact that Israel would not accept the dismantling of a single settlement in the Occupied Territories, and that if some settlements were under Palestinian sovereignty, they would have to be furnished with security arrangements acceptable to Israel. Israel also expects to maintain control over all of the roads and transportation to and from the settlements.

THE REAL PURPOSE OF THE SETTLEMENTS

Between 1967 and 1977, 35,000 Israelis settled in the Palestinian West Bank under the banner of God's commandment, with the support of the military machines of Israel and the United States, and with the backing of the industrial-military complex that benefited from tensions. The settlers did not exceed 1 percent of the population, and the religious among them were a minority. These were mostly pragmatic settlements, meant to control water resources and the main routes and borders in the Jordan Valley.

'God' had little to do with the cynical calculations of the Israeli Labor governments, but these soon became a pretext for religiously and economically motivated settlement in the Occupied Territories. On these grounds, a unifying body was established in the West Bank by the name of Yishaa, or the Council of Settlements in the West Bank and Gaza, or 'Judea Samaria and Hevel Gaza.' It was meant to support a certain autonomy for settlement action and expansion, and to better organize settlement viability and political representation. In the next decade, this body received a lot of help from the Likud governments.

For three decades, the central interest in maintaining the occupation and settlement of the Palestinian territories has been strategic and economic. After the 1967 war, the new borders provided strategic depth, especially where they are geographically more potent, such as the Jordan River or the Golan Heights. Moreover, within those borders, there are water resources and, eventually, there was cheap labor. According to one of Israel's leading experts on water and the Arab-Israeli conflict, Hebrew University Professor and US Department of Defense consultant, Haim Gvirtzman, Labor's settlement policy after 1967 followed specific guidelines that would insure Israel's total control over water resources in the West Bank. The map of the settlements looked like a hydraulic map of the territories. This allowed it to exploit over 500 million cubic meters of water out of the 600 million produced annually, which saved it at least US$1 billion a year from the territories it occupied in 1967, and satisfied an average of at least one-third of its water consumption. Except in small circles, the water argument was hardly ever mentioned, while theological arguments and religious symbols were continually invoked to justify control over land and the Jewish right to settle it.[4]

In order to maximize its profit, Israel pursued the 'Action of Time' approach whereby the longer Israel held the land, the more it would gain from it. This was conveniently maintained through collective symbols and religious sentiments, all of which were heightened by the interaction between the feeling aroused by the war and the encounter with the holy places, which were the cradle of Jewish mythology. Needless to say, the colonization of the land and annexation of parts of it excluded the original population because of the so-called 'demographic threat.'[5]

If the Israeli ideological machine was able to avoid the pre-1948 settlement of Palestinian land being labeled as colonization (the settlements were presented as simple, independent colonies – in contrast to the post-1948 ethnic cleansing that took place), the post-1967 occupation was a clear case of outright colonialism (for profit and exploitation) developed in concert wtih American policy in the Middle East.[6]

OSLO INSTITUTIONALIZES APARTHEID

In the last seven years, the absolute majority of the 2.7 million Palestinians living under Israeli rule was segregated from Israeli and Jewish settlers by security-imposed measures and arbitrary closures. The settlers had total liberty of movement in the Occupied Territories, while Palestinian liberty of movement was constrained by special permits given to those Palestinians who satisfied arbitrary Israeli conditions, or who were collaborators or elderly. For example, in 1994, after the Jewish settler, Baruch Goldstein, shot and killed twenty-nine Palestinians in Hebron, Israel confined 20,000 Hebron residents to their homes for two months because of their proximity to the Jewish settler community in the heart of Hebron, or the so-called H-2 area. Those settlers, meanwhile, were allowed to move around freely.

The overall security deployment in the Occupied Territories has erected barriers between communities and created more barbed-wired areas than ever before. The presence of some 200 military posts, including 100 military bases spread around 20 percent of the West Bank and 420 acres in Gaza, disrupted life in those territories. The Labor strategy of physical separation did not translate into equality, separation being no less than segregation. The logic of Oslo, which was underlined by Rabin's slogan 'Take Gaza out of Tel Aviv,' was reaffirmed by Barak's 'Us here, them over there.' Barak then added a malicious twist, 'economic separation,' which was immediately opposed by segments of the business community that has long profited from its economic relations with the Palestinians. Moreover, the fear of too high unemployment, poverty, and starvation, and hence instability and violence, blocked any further move on the idea of economic separation. Israel has barred independent development for the last thirty years, whether in electricity, water, or other essential services, and instead developed under-development under occupation.[7]

The cantonization of the territories through Jewish settlements and artificial army barriers has crippled the establishment of a viable economy or polity in Palestine. The northern canton includes Nablus, Jenin, and other towns; the central canton includes Ramallah and surrounding villages; the southern canton includes Bethlehem and part of Hebron, but Jericho would remain isolated, as does East Jerusalem in the West Bank; and of course Gaza in the south. This process was in violation of the Oslo agreement, which underlined the fact that these areas constitute 'a single territorial unit, whose integrity will be preserved during the interim phase.'

Closures have diminished the numbers of Palestinian laborers in Israel. Even when Israel pretended to open up the territories by agreeing to 'safe passage' between Gaza and the West Bank, Israeli negotiators insisted on enforcing the permit system, hence only allowing Palestinians to enter when it saw fit. Even family members who desire to visit any of the 3,000 political prisoners held in Israel have to go through hell in order to get a permit to go to Israel. The same holds true for those needing to work or study in East Jerusalem. Separate checkpoints for Bethlehem and East Jerusalem insure that separation will always remain a one-way segregation, as settlers and Israelis remain free to travel anywhere they desire.[8]

Israel hoped that these closures could indirectly contribute to the settlers' economy and insure the survival of the settlements as a guarantee of Israeli territorial expansion that would also facilitate the transformation of military control into economic domination. In this context, closures provided cheap Palestinian labor to the settlements and to the newly-established industrial parks, or Mequilladoras, on the edge of populated Palestinian centers. Violators of the ban on traveling to Israel could spend six months in jail and pay a fine of US$500. As a result, Palestinian labor has doubled in those settler enterprises, even though the wage of a Palestinian laborer in the settlements is far more degrading and is far lower than in Israel proper. A Palestinian laborer can earn up to $40 for an eight-hour day in Israel, or four times his earnings in the settlement, which are about $10 a day. Today, there are more than 100 Israeli enterprises in the settlements. In the industrial zone at the Ertez crossing between Gaza and Israel, 3,500 laborers are at work because of closures.[9]

Palestinian scholar Muhammad Hallaj accurately described this Israeli policy when he stated that 'Jewish settlements serve as the instrument of an apartheid system in the Occupied Territories. Their presence establishes and justifies pervasive discrimination in every aspect of life ... Arabs and Jews are governed under a dual system of law under which "non-Jews" are denied due process, equal protection of the law, and a whole range of rights and freedoms enjoyed by Jewish settlers. Jewish settlements in the West Bank and Gaza make Israel the only state in the world today where apartheid is the prevailing system of administration.'

Those unprotected cantons have been the victims of social, environmental, and economic discrimination. Increasingly, they have become the dumping ground of solid waste from Israel and the settlements. Cynically, the town of Abu Dis, whose name was invoked by the Israelis as a potential capital of the Palestinian state, has been used as an insanitary dumping site of waste from West Jerusalem. Israeli companies in such fields as medicine and paint have also used the West Bank as dumping grounds in the last several years. Moreover, Israel has moved many of its polluting industries to locations in the West Bank. Pesticides, fertilizer, aluminium, fiberglass, and plastic manufactures, at times banned in Israel, have relocated to the West Bank, according to Jad Issaq, director general of the Applied Research Institute in Jerusalem. Their waste water flows toward Palestinian villages with no control. The Israeli government has illegally constructed at least seven industrial zones that produce industrial waste, often polluting adjacent Palestinian lands.[10]

In summary, it is evident that Israel has exploited the vagueness in the Oslo agreement to legitimize its jurisdiction over 80 percent of the Occupied Territories and extend its domination to major facets of daily life including borders, land, water, and trade. It used this new 'legitimacy' to further separate itself from the Palestinians while suffocating their economy, making it dependent on the Israeli economy and settlements. The result: segregation and Apartheid.

GREATER ISRAEL – GREATER IMPASSE

SHARON AND THE SETTLEMENTS

During Ariel Sharon's visit to Washington on April 9, 1999 as minister of infrastructure, Secretary of State Albright asked him merely for a moratorium on settlement building, but was turned down. As he explained it to her, settlements were not obstacles to peace, but rather 'contribute to peace.' He sincerely believes it.

Sharon reckons that even the distant settlements must stay intact, as they will serve important goals once Israel finishes its expansion eastward. Between 1978 and 1981, Sharon established 240 settlements in Galilee in the West Bank, believing that they give Israel 'the depth it needs and the water sources and the essential strategic assets between the coastal plain and the Jordan River.' Accordingly, Sharon's map is well-known: 'an eastern security zone 10 to 20 kilometers wide and a western security zone 5 to 7 kilometers wide. And Jerusalem, of course. Above all, Jerusalem. And the main roads. The strategic points. The holy places of the Jewish people."[11]

Prime Minister Ariel Sharon admitted that without the settlements the army would have left long ago. Israeli leaders reckon they are the justification as to why Israelis 'don't see their military as a foreign army ruling a foreign population'. In 1977, when then-Minister Sharon chaired the ministerial committee for settlement affairs, he oversaw the establishment of new Jewish settlements in the West Bank and Gaza. He planned for settling 2 million Jews. A quarter of a century later, Prime Minister Sharon remains adamant that Israel has a 'moral' right to transform the demographics of these territories. Since his election in January 2001, Sharon has built 35 new settlement outposts (*New York Times*, April 27, 2002). In the mid 1970s, during the transition from Labor to Likud rule in Israel, Sharon emerged as the leader capable of realizing the dream of a 'Greater Land of Israel' beyond Israel's internationally recognized borders. Shimon Peres's encouragement to Israelis to settle 'everywhere' in the Occupied Territories strengthened Sharon's drive to implement the programme of the influential bipartisan Likud/Labor 'Greater Land of Israel' movement that foresaw an Israel spreading from the Jordan river to the Mediterranean. Twenty-five years after Sharon's plan went into effect, the number of settlers in the Occupied Territories outside East Jerusalem has jumped from 1,500 in 1972 to 7,000 in 1977 to nearly 100,000 in 1992. By 2002, over 200,000 settlers along with the army were occupying 59 percent of the West Bank, connected by some 350 km. of bypass roads. Combined with the settlers in East Jerusalem, they make up some 10 percent of Israel's Jewish population. A great number of these settlers are armed and dangerous fanatics with a shoot-to-kill license from the Israeli army.

In May 2000 Israeli settlers renewed their terrorist activities. Establishment of the settlements has undermined a peaceful solution to the occupation. When the army asked Sharon in May 2002 to remove a number of distant settlements and regroup them with better defended nearby settlement blocs, he dismissed the security-conscious proposal and vowed not to dismantle a single settlement while in office. Instead, Sharon brought in two new ministers from the National Religious Party (NRP) that make up the hardcore of the settlement leadership and made them members of his security cabinet overseeing the Occupied Territories.

There is no better way to describe the new geography of the settlements than to carve a map of the West Bank out a piece of fresh Swiss cheese. The small disconnected and empty black holes are the Palestinian cantons, called autonomous regions, and the surrounding continuous and rich yellow part constitutes the Jewish settlements. In recent years, frequent Israeli closures of the Palestinian communities have been particularly choking and disrupting for the inhabitants because they are imposed hermetically around towns and villages as well as at diverse locations in order to allow easy travel for the settlers. These settlement-motivated closures of Palestinian areas have been viewed by the International Monetary Fund (IMF) and the World Bank as more damaging to the Palestinian economy and its nation-building than any other cause.

The new generation settlers are nothing like their predecessors - the pre-1948 Mityashvim - who founded Zionism and shaped the state as a secular, socialist, predominantly European Jewish enterprise. The new post-1967 Mitnahlim settlers are predominantly religious, Reagan-style neo-conservatives. Moreover, and unlike their predecessors, their settlements are sponsored by the state of Israel. In order for pan-Israeli nationalism to succeed as it did for the 1948 settlers, the new Zionists (or post-Zionists) realize that they must finish the job with another campaign of ethnic cleansing, sooner rather than later. The newly appointed minister, Efi Eitam who also heads the NRP, sees a 'Greater Israel' as 'the state of God; the Jews are the soul of the world;

the Jewish people has a mission to reveal the image of God on earth'. He sees himself as standing 'in the same place that Moses and King David stood', where 'a world without Jews is a world of robots, a dead world; and the State of Israel is the Noah's Ark of the future of the world and its task is to uncover God's image' (Olek Netzer, *Haaretz*, April 28, 2002). Retired General Eitam, a settler-warrior who is the rising star of the settlement movement and the Religious Right, has admitted to the daily *Haaretz* that transfer is politically 'enticing', though not realistic without war. In case of violent conflict, such as the extension of the Intifada, the originally Laborite-minded general estimates that 'not many Arabs will remain'. A member of Sharon's inner security cabinet, Eitam called for war on Iraq and Iran through Israeli pre-emptive strikes (*Haaretz*, April 12, 2002).

During a recent tour of the West Bank with a group of European civil rights activists, we encountered an American settler who spoke to us of his glorious days in the civil rights movement in America. Asked if that did not contradict with his colonial crusade in the Palestinian territories, he referred us to the Torah. When told that it was the Afrikaners of South Africa who spoke of themselves as 'a distinct people, occupying a distinct fatherland, speaking a God-given language and endowed by God with the destiny to rule [the land] and civilize its heathen peoples', the peaceful exchange turned violent as stones were hurled at our bus. Even Israel's friends in the West have said that if the logic of the settlers wins, Israel would be transformed into an Apartheid state (see Thomas Friedman and others in American journals). For former-Intelligence Chief Ami Ayalon, characteristics of Apartheid are real already. Former Israeli Attorney-General Michael Ben-Yair reckons the logic of the fundamentalist settlers has already won as Israel has 'established an Apartheid regime in the Occupied Territories' (*Haaretz*, March 3, 2002).

THE CANCER OF ISRAELI SETTLEMENTS

Throughout the years, low- and middle-income families and new immigrants were enticed to move into the settlements by offers of cheap housing and financial reward, at times using American aid money. But as the promise of better living turned into a colonial nightmare, the pragmatic settlers tilted ideologically towards the Right. More than 94 percent voted for Binyamin Netanyahu and Ariel Sharon in recent elections. Today, the fanatic fundamentalist settlers dictate the mood in the umbrella council that oversees the settlements and they exercise a formidable influence over decision-making in the Israeli government. Although for the international community they constitute extra-territorial entities, the settlements are a hotbed of pan-Israel nationalism driven by religious fervour and motivated by the promise of conquering new frontiers.

Unlike those Israelis who seek an internationally recognized 'Jewish state' within sovereign borders, the new zealots insist that their homeland is the 'Land of Israel', not the 'state of Israel' and, therefore, will not allow the emergence of another state between the river and the sea. Moreover, the power of the settlers goes beyond their electoral influence and into the heart of political decision-making. Over the last quarter century, with the exception of the short-lived Rabin and Barak governments, the religious settlers' influence increased rapidly as a political hardcore of the Likud/religious coalitions governed Israel. They are not only a menace to Palestine and to a normalized Israel, but also to the whole region.

A quick look at the thinking emerging from their newly set-up strategic think-tanks in the settlements shows a war-driven thinking that taps on new American concepts such as the 'War on Terrorism', 'Axis of Evil', new missile systems, and the worst sensationalist literature the Pentagon produces. As the settlers go on to implement America's war Israeli-style, coexistence with their next-door neighbours is anything but on their mind. The Jewish religious fundamentalists in the Occupied Territories believe that 'Israel is the hope of the world', while 'Palestinian moral savagery is organized to prevent this'. Paradoxically, the Palestinian suicide bombings have played into the settlers' hands. The settlers' erroneous claim that the Palestinians are interested not only in their removal, but also in that of Israel, has shifted the pressure away from the settlements as obstacles to peace, into radicalizing the entire Israeli society, making it even more susceptible to settler ideology.

Settlements are the reason for Israel's closures on each and every Palestinian camp and urban centre. Temporary closures have been even more inhumane and disruptive to Palestinian life and development as tanks rather than agreements draw the borderlines. The occupation is affecting Israel no less. As it is plunged into fear and uncertainty, religious fundamentalism and radical Jewish nationalism are taking hold of the country. The settler ideology has been eating into Israel's pluralistic politics even as it swallows more Palestinian land. The settler groups have become ever more influential in the Israeli establishment and army as settlements become the most damaging obstacle to peace. The settlements are radicalizing Israeli society. Already ten members of the Israeli Knesset are settlers and all belong to Sharon's governing coalition. As stated earlier, three served as ministers and two are serving as deputy ministers in his cabinet. These mostly religious fundamentalists could not care less about Palestinian reform or international norms of conduct. Today, 30 fundamentalist religious legislators, or a quarter of the Knesset, support Sharon's extra-territorial settlement policy.

Settlers and religious fundamentalists are against any withdrawal from the Occupied Territories or the dismantling of a single settlement. They also believe that international law is not applicable in the case of the Occupied Territories, territories they consider their heritage. The adoption in May 2002 of Netanyahu's populist proposal in the Likud Party against a Palestinian state has shown the strength of the settlers and radical nationalists in the governing party. Consider the two stark settlement examples of Nitzarim in the Gaza strip and Romema inside Hebron on the West Bank. The latter has an army division to protect it and to disrupt the lives of thousands of Palestinians, and the former, an illegal home for 40 Israeli families in the impoverished sea of Palestinian refugees, has led to the deaths of dozens of Palestinians and at least 15 Israeli soldiers. Israeli measures protecting the settlers' expansion has transformed the autonomous territories into eight big prison cells. Mounting deprivation, oppression, and daily humiliation will only fuel the fires of revenge and conflict and undermine attempts at reconciliation. In the process, more suicide bombings and terrorism have been forthcoming from Palestinians, as well as terrorism from the settlers.

Sharon has further reinforced a dual system in the West Bank and Gaza. There is an expanding one for the 200 settlements connected through bypass roads and separate development that is superior to the ever-shrinking system for the indigenous population in less than half of the West Bank, which lacks any geographic continuity and is subservient to the settlers' interests. This is Apartheid. So dangerous is the Apartheid-generated thinking of radical nationalists that the option of ethnic cleansing remains viable in the long term, once coexistence under Israeli domination does not work. Another transfer like that of 1948 is looming on the horizon of Israeli politics, even if it does not pose a real or immediate threat. As settlers dig deep into the land and are more frequently faced with Palestinian hostility, the leaders of the National Union (NU), NRP, and the Russian-based Yisraeli Biteno parties, who cannot foresee an Israeli withdrawal of the settlers, propose instead a 'transfer of the Palestinians' to neighboring countries, preferably peacefully, but violently if necessary. According to this view, Sharon could exploit the next confrontation or war to effect a final solution of sorts to the Palestinian problem. According to one Israeli source, 150,000 Palestinians, or 10 percent of the West Bank population, have left the Occupied Territories since the start of this second Intifada.

THE ENDGAME

All the evidence shows that the Israelis' settlement drive policy continued regardless of signed agreements, and eventually became the principal engine of violence in the Occupied Territories as they created a new geography of conflict that hampered Palestinian development and undermined peace. Today millions of Palestinians and Israelis continue to live in fear for the sake of illegal settlers who are plunging the area into communal/colonial war. If Israel continues to expand settlement activity as it did during the peace process, the number of settlers will climb to a million. In that case, separating Palestinians from Israel and its settlers will be impossible without ethnic cleansing. Barbed wire and electronic sensors will not be able to segregate the Palestinians for long, while the geography that separates them keeps on shrinking. Paradoxically, not only will the future of a Palestinian state be compromised, but also the chances for maintaining a Jewish state or Jewish majority will diminish in Mandate Palestine (Israel, the West Bank, and Gaza) as the nine million Israeli Jews and Palestinian Arabs become increasingly inseparable. For now, the logic of Sharon and his settlers will continue to underline a state of permanent conflict and war in Palestine and the Middle East. Unless the international community intervenes, the settlers' logic will eventually lead to the same standoff that occurred on the eve of the 1948 war: either accept a bi-national state or attempt another ethnic cleansing. Already the 'Transfer', or the collective expulsion of the Palestinians, is on the minds and lips of many members of Sharon's cabinet. This time around, however, such a crime would be a dramatic strategic error for Israel, considering what became of Milosovic.

NOTES

1. 'Statistical Abstract of Israel 1992–1999,' *Peace Now*, December 5, 1999.

2. *Report on Israeli Settlements*, July–August, 1999, and

September–October, 1999, Foundation for Middle East Peace, Washington, DC.

3. Don Peretz, 'The 1998 Wye River Memorandum: An Update,' Summary, 29 July 1999, Center for Policy Analysis on Palestine, Washington, DC.

4. Noam Chomsky, *World Orders Old and New*, Columbia University Press, New York, 1996, pp. 210–213.

5. Baruq Kimmerling, *Zionism and Territory*, University of California Press, 1993.

6. Gershon Shafir, *Journal of Palestine Studies*, Washington, Vol. XXV, No. 3 (Spring 1996), pp. 24–25.

7. In contrast, the Palestinian territories exported almost ten times more valued goods to Jordan than they imported from it, or US$1.46 billion to $150 million in the first twenty-two years of occupation.

8. Allegra Pacheco, 'Closure and Apartheid: Seven Years of "Peace" through Separation,' *Information Brief* No. 6, March, 2000, CPAP, Washington DC.

9. 'Report on the Settlements,' September/October 1999, Foundation for Middle East Peace, Washington, DC.

10. Jad Issac, *Information Brief* No. 14, March, 2000, CPAP, Washington DC.

11. Ari Shavit, 'Israel according to Sharon,' *Haaretz*, February 2, 2001.

NO END IN SIGHT

9

BETRAYAL

The Oslo Peace Process was a sham. It was transformed into a diplomatic circus as soon as it was signed. The international community looked on amazed as the American magician pulled one agreement after another from his sleeve, while the besieged Palestinians had their one moment in the limelight. There were more than a few carrots to go around as long as there were agreements to be signed. Seven years later, the bunny was tired of jumping, the money was running out, and the magician's spectacle was becoming repetitive and, frankly, embarrassing. Like all melodramas, the theatrics of Oslo ended with tears of laughter and pain. It reduced the Palestinian question - one of the most just and dramatic causes of the century - into one of endless cheating, wheeling, and dealing. The theft of a whole homeland rendering half its people refugees and the rest under occupation was reduced to real-estate bickering and demand for cool-headed reform under the heat of the military incursions. The victims have been blamed for their victimization and were coerced to honor and protect their victimizer.

The Palestinian people were betrayed in the most fundamental way by a process that promised to set them free. They gave it their best; patiently and tolerantly they built schools and public institutions and invested in their future despite Israel's obstacles and their leaders' corruption. They watched helplessly as a zero-sum process passed them by: Israelis became richer and they became poorer, Israel expanded and Israelis circulated freely as their territory shrank as they were incarcerated within their cantons. The more friends and allies they lost in the international arena, the more Israel picked up new diplomatic relations.

After seven hard years and seven unsavory bilateral accords, an uneasy feeling of injustice reigned in Palestine. Palestinians felt that the goal of a lasting peace was being substituted by a lasting peace process. With the consent and bankrolling of Western institutions, Israel carved Palestine up into bantustans, referred to in the alphabetic diplomatic jargon as areas A, B, C, H1, and H2. Meanwhile Kosovo, East Timor, and other nations acquired their right to self-determination as independent states with the help of the international community. The Palestinians were still under occupation after 35 years. Refugees in different continents of the world made their way home while the Palestinians lingered in their camps under Israeli bombardment. Many were made refugees all over again after the destruction of their homes. Young Palestinian refugees in Jenin, Balata, Al-Ama'ari, and other refugee camps were groomed by Israeli bombardment into the new generation of the Palestinian Nakba, or Catastrophe. An immune Israel dismissed one UN Security Council resolution after another, even as other resolutions were implemented by military means and economic sanctions elsewhere in the world. The United States refused to step in and Europe would not interfere, each citing its own pitiful excuses for allowing international law and universal values to be violated. The Palestinians were abandoned by fellow nations to the wrath of vengeful Israeli generals.

Palestinians of all classes and ages took to the streets in protest against the transformation of a brutal occupation into a system of Apartheid by a paradoxically powerful and paranoid, brutal and vulnerable Israel. The deeper the international betrayal, the bloodier the occupation, the more violent became the Intifada. Surrounded by an incapacitated and paralysed Arab world and a divided Europe, besieged and desperate Palestinian cries for freedom and independence fell on deaf ears in both the West and the East. Palestinians have mostly remained steadfast and continued to reject their dehumanization by Israeli occupation. The Palestinians' refusal to lose, in spite of their great losses, made Israel's victory impossible. They mostly went on resisting the occupation in one form or another. A few went on to die. Carrying out their suicide bombings against mostly innocent Israeli civilians, young Palestinians have derailed the conflict with Israel into the place Israeli leaders hoped it would be: within the context of the 'War on Terrorism'. But while dozens went on to suicide, millions of Palestinians remained determined to live in honor and freedom.

The international community might be expected to say 'enough is enough', but no. Washington persists with its incremental approach, defying all international norms and blocking international intervention, thus allowing Israel to break the will of a brave people.

Nine years after the ill-fated architect of Oslo, Shimon Peres, promised a new dawn in the Middle East, he called for establishing another 'peace process', in other words, another 'tunnel' that would enable us to see the light at the end of it. He also called upon a hesitant Europe to 'come out of the closet' and openly declare its allegiance to America's policy. This is Nobel Prize material. Neither Israel nor America nor Europe accepted responsibility for the regress of the process and for breaking their promises and cheating the Palestinian people out of their liberty. Worse, they blamed a weak Palestinian Authority (PA), partly their own creation, for their cynicism and their mistakes. In fact, the responsibility falls squarely on their shoulders for allowing Israel to continue lowering Oslo's political ceiling until they all had to bend down to keep up.

LESSONS FROM OSLO

The peace process nurtured Palestinian dependence on Israel instead of independence from it. It led to more 'Jewish settlements' instead of a 'peace settlement'. It sanctioned more bypass roads, more land confiscation, and more house demolitions. It also resulted in further economic decline, increased unemployment, and less stability in the West Bank and Gaza. Hailed as a success in the diplomatic arena, the peace process has proved, in fact, to be a total failure by any international norms of conflict resolution. In Israel, both Labor and Likud governments have tried for years to undermine a legal partition solution by offering different formulas based on separation/segregation. Palestinian scholar Hisham Sharabi summarized the Israeli policy toward the peace process as follows:

> While Rabin's formula was based on a streamlined version of the South African bantustan model, with limited self-rule in the guise of a Palestinian state, Netanyahu's plan was based on an antiquated apartheid model with local autonomy but without even a vestige of statehood. Thus, the disagreement between Labor and Likud has not been over substance, as the mainstream media maintains, since both reject partition, but over a politically correct way of segregating the Palestinians within a framework that will preserve Israel's hegemony over all of Palestine.

No wonder the Labor party joined a Sharon government with little quarrel over its agenda. No Israeli leader during or before Oslo envisioned sharing the land with the Palestinian people as equals, or as a nation aspiring to self-determination within the same land, their own land. They were under no pressure to do so, because Israeli impunity in the international community, especially since the advent of Oslo, has allowed Israel to continue to ignore international law and legitimacy and enticed it to undermine signed agreements when its narrow interests were not served. The amelioration of business conditions in Israel and the prospering Israeli business community relieved it of any economic pressure to end its system of Apartheid. It is ironic that the same Oslo process that institutionalized Israeli racism in Palestine has also paved the way for successful American-Israeli efforts to repeal the repeatedly affirmed UN resolution equating Zionism with racism. In other words there was no compelling reason why Israel needed to produce its own F.W. de Klerk. In South Africa, economic pressure and a growing sense of realism impelled de Klerk to release African National Congress (ANC) leader Nelson Mandela, dismantle Apartheid, and begin the process of creating a new, multiracial South Africa. Israel, on the other hand, is not ready to decolonize. Whether or not Arafat is a Palestinian Mandela is irrelevant in the absence of an Israeli de Klerk or de Gaulle, who could put an end once and for all to Apartheid and occupation.

ISRAEL'S ZERO-SUM POLICY

At the end of the day, it became clear that the Israelis were not ready for a historic compromise with the Palestinians. They were only looking for a truce that would allow them further domination. Technically, Israeli leaders offered the Palestinians two options but no real solution. The younger, more arrogant Barak and Netanyahu insisted on 'final' agreements that would end the conflict and put an end to Palestinian claims. But they wanted this without budging on their common red lines: notably, no return of the refugees, no return to the 1967 borders, and no sovereign Palestinian state in the West Bank and Gaza with East Jerusalem as its capital. On the other side, the older, more experienced, and cynical Peres and Sharon planned, each in his own way, for 'long-term' agreements that would address certain issues, but prolong or postpone others indefinitely, while occupation and settlement continued. In both cases, Israel accepted the principle of a Palestinian state - but only once it was emptied of its meaning.

Ironically, once the second Intifada erupted, Israeli Jews felt ghettoized by their own cantonization of the Palestinians. Once Palestinian solidarity and protest inside Israel emerged in solidarity with Palestinians under occupation and in the refugee camps, Israel changed its security buffer from the Occupied Territories to the Arab regions in Israel proper. The Israeli Arab populated region of the Triangle, not far from Tel Aviv, was treated in the same way as the autonomous Area A in the West Bank (i.e. only partially under Palestinian control). The Intifada made the Israelis feel that their Apartheid system had gone awry. Overwhelmed by Palestinian anger, the Israelis responded with more violence. Hence, Israeli society empowered Ariel Sharon, a general with a long record of massacres and bloodshed, to take the reins of government. His utterance that 'the war has been going on for 120 years' and that Israel will 'triumph' has called forth the specter of renewed Israeli ethnic cleansing in Palestine.

Sharon's genie came out with an alternative logic to Oslo. His 'peace through security' - proven a failure since 1948 - translated into undermining attempts at achieving 'security through peace', or negotiations. Sharon's political endgame after 'badly beating the Palestinians' is a humiliating proposal that envisions half a Palestinian state on half of the West Bank and Gaza, but only in the long run.

At the time of writing, diplomatic efforts are concentrating on a plan to allow the Palestinians a discontinuous 'state' in areas A and B that make up 42 percent of the West Bank, or less than 10 percent of Palestine. After that the state of Palestine will negotiate on the rest of the issues. Risible as this may seem, the fact that the Arab parties are considering it is catastrophic. Today, the only alternative Israeli vision to Sharon's occupation and Apartheid is coming from Israel's old securitarian Labor mould of Allon, Moshe Dayan, and Yitzhak Rabin. It calls for unilateral separation from the Palestinians or 'unilateral withdrawal' from parts or most of the occupied West Bank and Gaza and erecting new walls with the Palestinians. This will also translate into segregation in the absence of recognized international borders. The most vocal spokesman of this camp has been the former head of the intelligence community in Israel, Ami Ayalon, but Ehud Barak has also proposed pulling out of 75 percent, leaving two huge security strips east and west of the West Bank. His idea of separation from the Palestinians is based strictly on Israel's perceived security and demographic concerns. It will require the building of a wall, Berlin-style, already begun, to achieve this goal.

At best, Israelis are ready to accept some kind of Palestinian state, but one that is dependent on Israel with compromised sovereignty. They are willing to accept a state that is a product of

Israeli 'generosity' and 'hurtful compromises', rather than the result of an Israeli admission of the historical and legitimate Palestinian right to the land. They will accept a state defined by Israel's security needs and constrained by its self-defined national imperatives, rather than by the security and wellbeing of the new state itself. Even the so-called far-reaching Barak proposals are limited to this national Israeli consensus that is ready to recognize an expanded autonomy as a state.

A Palestinian state is the one possible outcome of a viable and just resolution of the conflict, it cannot be an alternative to it. That means an end to occupation and the withdrawal of all Israelis, soldiers and settlers, in order to allow the Palestinians the opportunity to practice their right to self-determination in a state. A virtual state cannot be an alternative to complete Israeli withdrawal.

PALESTINIAN INTIFADA LACKS STRATEGY

The Palestinians have been ready for nearly three decades to reach a historic reconciliation based on the 1967 borders and the recognition by Israel of their Right of Return. The Palestine Liberation Organization (PLO) made a historic compromise when it recognized the Israeli state, comprising over three-quarters of the Palestinians' historical homeland, and gave de facto recognition to Israel's capital on more than two-thirds of Jerusalem occupied in 1967, all done at the opening of the Oslo process. A costly compromise indeed.

At the Camp David summit, the Palestinians agreed to more compromises. They accepted the principle of land swaps, and at Taba they provided maps for it with an exchange of roughly 3.1 percent. They also accepted a demilitarized state on less than one-fifth of their land.

In February 2002, Arafat wrote in the *New York Times* that while the Right of Return must be recognized, its implementation should take Israeli demographics into consideration.

Any further compromise will be met with scorn and rejection by the Palestinians and will lead to failure. The Palestinians' yearning for self-determination and independence has been compromised by an economically dependent relationship vis-à-vis Israel, and the pursuit of sovereignty tainted by the absence of accountability and democracy in the Palestinian-controlled enclaves. Before Oslo, the Palestinian territories were a 'whole', despite the occupation. After 1993, they were divided and sub-divided into separate bantustans. Israel dominated the overall security arrangements and curtailed the Palestinians' freedom of movement even within the Occupied Territories. It has disrupted daily living and torn asunder family relations; it has weakened the national bond, the sense of community, the organizational structures, and all other societal relations among Palestinians and towards their land. All this has facilitated more nepotism and corruption. The overpopulated and miserable Gaza Strip - Arafat's power base - consists of 80 percent refugees; these people are capable of distinguishing between a red line and a white flag. For them, Israel's refusal to take moral and legal responsibility for the refugees, to give back Jerusalem, or to renounce its racist system of Apartheid will be a non-starter in terms of the implementation of a 'final agreement'.

THE SECOND INTIFADA AND BEYOND
– THE ACTORS AND THE ACTION

The second Intifada, like previous uprisings, was a direct and inescapable result of continued merciless occupation. The people who took to the streets were not acting on orders. This was a very spontaneous reaction to Israeli threats, ultimatums, and use of excessive force. In fact, most of Arafat's cabinet was unhappy with the outbreak of violence. Whether it was a question of their collective investments or their personal wealth and special VIP status, at the end of the day the Palestinian leadership and its cronies had much to lose from the Intifada. Luckily, except in a few cases, Arafat refused to do Israel's bidding and crack down on the Intifada, which would have led to civil conflict among his people while Israel looked on. It would have been astonishing if Palestinians, as an occupied people, were not to revolt.

Barak's modus operandi raised the stakes of the Intifada, making it impossible for the Palestinians to back down without clear results. The tenacity of Palestinian youth in the West Bank and Gaza, as well as within Israel itself, succeeded in unmasking the true nature of Israeli colonialism. It showed that, as long as it remained a colonial power, Israel could not pretend to be a democracy, and that Apartheid is no alternative to peace in Palestine.

The Palestinian Authority was forced to accept the consequences - the spilling of the innocent blood of Palestinians - and rejected Israeli demands to curtail the Intifada by force. Regardless of whether this has been an Intifada of *tahrir* (liberation) or *tahrik* (to stir or shake), it attempted to accomplish what the interim diplomatic process had failed to do: the evacuation of Israeli forces from the West Bank with the exception of the big settlement blocs, or from 90 percent of the Occupied Territories as stipulated by the Oslo process. Indeed, the Intifada succeeded after only two months in disrupting the daily life of Jewish settlers in the West Bank and Gaza, and the road networks they had built during Oslo, thereby interrupting the settlement drive.

But while the goal of the Intifada revolved around freedom, equality, and independence, the means used to reach those honorable ends were not up to the task. Suicide bombings have harmed the Palestinians. Non-violent resistance would have been the best and most productive path to take. Also, restricting resistance to within the 1967 borders could have had important political results and earned the Palestinians more international support in the long run. But as the situation continued to deteriorate under Sharon's war machine, some Palestinians concluded differently. In other words, the massive demonstrations began to give way to covert operations against the army and settlers; these operations later took the form of suicide bombings inside Israel itself in the hope that the majority of Israelis would conclude that occupation and Apartheid does not pay.

Once both peoples tire of violence, Israel will have to commit itself to withdrawing its army from the Occupied Territories and dismantling Apartheid. That is when serious negotiations could begin. And yet, terrorism should not be accepted as the weapon of the weak. International legality and justice are the weak's best allies. Suicide bombings cannot achieve justice. Former Prime Minister Ehud Barak, Israel's most decorated general, once remarked that had he been born a Palestinian he would have become a terrorist. Fortunately, most of Palestinian youth continues to search for life. Only through strengthening the hope of a decent standard of living can we overcome the culture of hatred and death. Occupation, on the other hand, is said to be Israel's only means of protecting its security. It is not: the occupation is Israel's worst enemy. Palestinian resistance to this occupation will no doubt continue until all Israeli forces have withdrawn.

OCCUPATION vs SUICIDE BOMBINGS

Nonetheless, Palestinian suicide bombings, the resort of a minority, not to mention legitimate resistance, should not be compared to the 35-year brutal occupation, the real engine of violence in the area. Western media have all too often referred to Israeli practices as retaliations and acts of defense, or at best drawn parallels or moral equivalences between Israeli aggression and Palestinian resistance or suicide bombings. They have not explained the difference between permanent military occupation and legitimate resistance. They have not distinguished between actions committed on the one hand by an elected government of a member-state of the UN, which is required to abide by the UN's charter and conventions, and those of underground Palestinian groups and individuals living under occupation. Western observers should note that Islamist groups Hamas and Jihad do not have commercial agreements with Western countries, do not play basketball in Europe or join in Eurovision as Israel does. Israeli officials feel at home in modern Europe, while their policies are taken from chapters of the darkest days of

Apartheid and colonialism. Israel cannot claim to belong to the liberal democracies and at the same time be excused for creating two categories of citizens, one Jewish, one Arab, and for violating international law and, particularly, the Fourth Geneva Convention of 1949 regulating the conduct of an occupying force. And yet, Sharon's Israel continues cruelly to segregate villages and towns and cut them off with impassable barriers. Its army persists in using all the force at its disposal to oppress Palestinians eager for liberty and dignity after suffering decades of colonialism and violence. Undoing the occupation remains the only way out of the cycle of violence, and a good start to negotiating a final peace agreement.

TO ACHIEVE PEACE: WHAT TO DO AND WHAT NOT TO DO

Despite failures of Oslo, all new local and Western initiatives and plans seem to repeat the mistakes of the past. In order for any future negotiated agreement, whether long-term or final, to be successful and to withstand the test of time, it must depend, not on the balance of power, as Oslo did, but rather on international legality, justice, and guaranteed implementation. In Israel/Palestine, political commitments to justice and coexistence, rather than coerced diplomatic solutions, are viable in the long term. In this respect, Israel's 'red lines' are in direct violation of international law. 'No' to the return to 1967 borders means 'no' to UN Security Council Resolution 242. 'No' to the return of Palestinian refugees means 'no' to UN Security Council Resolution 194. 'No' to withdrawal from East Jerusalem and to Palestinian sovereignty over it means 'no' to UN Resolutions 242 and 181. 'No' to the dismantling of Jewish settlements built on the Occupied Territories means 'no' to UN Resolution 242 and 'no' to the 4th Geneva Convention. The Palestinian red lines reflect the opposite. They call for the full application of the international resolutions that have long been ignored by Israel, particularly since Washington took the peace process out of its international framework. Moreover, an agreement must contain the full legal separation of the two territories, and the recognition of Palestinian sovereignty, if it is to be practical and realizable. In the absence of such a clear legal framework, Israel will end up militarily encircling Palestine from all sides (including the Jordan river - another Israeli red line), and will instead strengthen the Apartheid system already in place.

As this book goes to print, Washington and Israel continue to push for Palestinian security guarantees to protect Israel's occupation and settlements, while the Palestinians themselves are ever more oppressed, weak, and vulnerable. Such tactics have not only been tried and failed, but are a scandalous waste of time and life. International legitimacy and fairness aside, the seven years of Oslo have taught the Palestinians and the Arabs that Israel's application of any agreement, temporary or final, is an excruciating challenge. If the legal clauses and the final goal of a given agreement are not crystal clear, the Palestinian leadership will have to confront a skeptical population that has little to lose by opposing it, money notwithstanding. For the Palestinians, a referendum on an agreement that defines their future homeland, and turns the page on their disheartening past, is far more urgent than a proposed Israeli referendum renouncing an illegal occupation. That is why a referendum among Palestinians, all Palestinians including the 3.7 million registered refugees, is a necessary prerequisite for the ratification of any final agreement signed in Washington. Otherwise we can only expect more Intifadas.

The only path to peace is for Israel to abide by international law and by its own signed agreements. This does not necessarily mean the use or threat of force. Over the years, the only time there was progress was when Israel was pressured into it by the international community, especially the United States. Such pressure strengthens the country's badly needed peace camp. Lifting its American-imposed immunity in the UN Security Council and taking away its freedom to act with impunity can only serve the principles of de-colonialization - a prerequisite for stability and peace - and, hence, serve both Israeli and Palestinian security. Helping the Palestinians to exercise their right to self-determination in their own state is the only way to reach historic reconciliation between the two peoples.

A total halt to the settlements as stated by the Mitchell Commission must be implemented. Israeli settlements are the greatest barrier to achieving peace in the Middle East; they are the raison d'etre and the engine of Israeli occupation of Palestinian territories. Despite three decades of American and European objections to their construction, rapid expansion of illegal Israeli settlements has undermined all Palestinian attempts at nation building. Their proliferation will bring about a costly end to the Israel envisioned by its founders. The settlement drive and ideology has in recent years become a cornerstone of the modern Israeli national identity that can best be defined as theological and adventurist. The settlement-driven politics of Sharon's government, with its violent manifestations, have bypassed ethnic and religious divides in Israel to mould a new 'Israelism' based not on the citizenship of diverse Jewish and Palestinian communities, but defined by colonial Jewish nationalism.

The settlers and their allies are reproducing Israel according to their own image: a theocracy in permanent conflict. Under Sharon's rule, and with the explicit support of the Bush administration, this process is increasingly becoming an irreversible and destructive self-fulfilling prophecy. Ending the occupation is indispensable for instituting a real democratic process and empowering the Palestinians to make Arafat and the rest of the PA accountable for charges of corruption, nepotism, and other misdeeds. It is also needed to normalize life in Israel and allow the Palestinians to exercise their right to self-determination. Determining the self collectively translates into sovereignty and citizenship. Only then can individual self- determination be carried out in the context of a free and open democratic process. Putting an end to Israeli Apartheid can pave the way for a process of Palestinian democratization and reform, not the other way around.

ONE STATE - TWO STATES

At the end of the day, there are two options for Israelis and Palestinians: either they live in two separate states with one form of relationship or another (for example, with Jordan, in confederation, or as Two States-One Holy Land, etc.), or in one state with one sort of constitution or another that could accommodate both peoples (examples are Canada, Switzerland, Belgium, etc.). No other realistic option exists in the medium term. Apartheid and ethnic cleansing are not options in Palestine. For further information, Israel can check with de Klerk and Milosevic. But whatever the arrangement might be, there should be fewer walls erected and more openings encouraged.

At the beginning of the new century, the entire Palestinian population in the West Bank and Gaza lives at a maximum distance of six miles from Israeli-controlled territories - including 400,000 settlers and 202 Palestinian cantons. In the overall territory of Palestine/Israel there are, according to Palestinian statistics, almost 4.5 million Palestinians and 4.5 million Jews. Hence, there are two durable ways for Palestinians to coexist with Israelis in peace: either they are granted the right to self-determination in their own sovereign state in the territories occupied in 1967, including East Jerusalem, or they are naturalized in the state of Israel/Palestine alongside the one million Palestinian Israeli citizens, in a bi-national or liberal democratic state with 'one person, one vote'.

Any further delay in resolving the outstanding issues and establishing a Palestinian state will only reinforce the existing Apartheid, eventually leading to a bi-national entity. In short, Israelis have a choice: either they address the long-evaded dilemma of their state's existence (i.e., the establishment of Israel on the ruins of another nation, the Palestinians, who have been scattered in exile, under occupation and under direct Israeli sovereignty); or polarization and discrimination will deepen the antagonism of the Apartheid system already in place. Already, reports of segregation, not only in the West Bank but also within Israel, are on the increase. On the beaches, in children's playgrounds, and in amusement parks,

Israeli police have been harassing Palestinians who come close to Jewish areas, at times under the pretext that only residents are allowed. Last, but not least, if Israel continues to enjoy impunity in the context of America's 'war against terrorism', the conflict will probably continue to escalate. It will tumble from accord to confrontation and from handshake to hostility.

The Israeli and American cynics are already lined up with their future perspectives about a region that, according to their analysis, has a limited choice between 'peace with violence' or outright war that will involve, as mounting numbers of Israeli officials claim, another transfer of Palestinians to outside their homeland. Israel's use of force has lost its logic in the absence of more territories to conquer and with the refusal of the Palestinians to give up their liberty. Israel must begin to evolve into a normal state, one that is willing to live under equitable peace and justice with the Palestinians. So why not begin now? Israel could stop the violence and make a historic apology to the Palestinian people. It needs only to realize that a peaceful relationship between Israelis and Palestinians is no longer a zero-sum game where Palestinian gains translate into Israeli losses or vice versa.

If they choose to separate, a strong and viable Palestinian state could be a legitimate partner in peace and stability. If they choose to integrate, a democratic Israel/Palestine, liberal or bi-national, could revolutionize the region and reinvent its economic and social relations, allowing both peoples to partake of milk and honey.

In my opening Introduction, I shared with you how my class of 2001 reached an agreement in a simulation exercise of the negotiations. Sadly, after one year of Sharon and Bush and the Intifada, my class of 2002 could no longer agree. Influenced by the dramatic evolution of the conflict, my students failed to reach a peaceful accord. Instead they set up a peace club at the university. As I watch the hard reality of Palestine unfold, I am more convinced than ever that a real peace movement is needed today; a peace movement is more important than a virtual peace process, in the region as well as internationally, in order to exercise sufficient pressure on the parties to come to an agreement. It is South Africa all over again.

I shall end on a personal note. Both peoples need to hold onto dreams of a common and prosperous future and give up past dreams of exclusivity over the land. Israelis need to underline diversity and shun racism, and one day the Palestinians will need to forgive. If the two should separate, let it be only a temporary step on the way to integration. It is perhaps the destiny of the two peoples to live together. If not, then let their divorce be a fair and civilized one.

INDEX

